THE

HISTORIC STYLES

OF

ORNAMENT

CONTAINING 1500 EXAMPLES FROM ALL COUNTRIES

AND ALL PERIODS, EXHIBITED ON

ONE HUNDRED PLATES

MOSTLY PRINTED IN GOLD AND COLOURS

WITH

HISTORICAL AND DESCRIPTIVE TEXT,

TRANSLATED FROM THE GERMAN OF H. DOLMETSCH.

LONDON

B. T. BATSFORD, 94 HIGH HOLBORN.

1898.

Printed by Hoffmann. Stuttgart.

LIST OF PLATES.

INDEX.

PREFACE.

The rise of technical education is everywhere accompanied by an increasing interest in the art productions of ancient and modern times, and a thorough knowledge of the different styles of ornament becomes more and more necessary to all designers and Art workers.

The aim of this publication is to meet this need. It is not intended to set forth theoretical precepts, but to serve as a practical guide, showing by a series of examples chronologically arranged, how, in succeeding epochs, Ornament, and especially the application of colour to it, developed in various countries.

In compiling it my object has been specially directed to the classification of such prominent and characteristic types as are most suitable for systematic study; and to supply Art Workers, from whom the fickle taste of our time constantly requires new forms, with a Treasury in which they can find valuable suggestions for working out original designs

Thanks to those who have aided in forming this collection by placing at my disposal objects of Art, and original drawings, and also owing to the material collected during my travels, I am fortunately able to illustrate many examples hitherto unpublished.

It has been my endeavour to give, as far as possible, the exact titles of the books from which illustrations have been borrowed, in order to direct those desirous of further examining special styles to the most helpful works illustrating them.

It is hoped that this third edition, increased by the addition of 15 plates and 136 illustrations in the text, may meet with a cordial reception, and prove useful to all who may examine its contents.

October, 1897.

H. Dolmetsch.

Plate 1.

EGYPTIAN.

PAINTING AND PLASTIC ART.

The mode of decoration with the Egyptians, the most ancient of civilized nations, comprises symbolic figure-subjects chiefly in conjunction with hieroglyphics. Columns and walls were used to write thereon a pictorial chronicle of religious and every-day-life. The figural representations on the outer walls of Egyptian buildings consist of very flat, frequently painted reliefs, called coilanaglyphs. The contours are deep cut, the object is treated plastically, but in such a way, that the most prominent parts remain equal to the surface of the wall. Plate 1 Fig. 1. The paintings themselves are carried out in flat tints without any modelling at all, they have sharp contours and show a rich and harmonious combination of colours.

From the vegetable and animal kingdoms in Egyptian ornamentation the most frequently employed are: the lotus flower, (an attribute of Isis and a symbol of the generating power of nature); the Nymphaea, the papyrus, the reed etc.; moreover the ram, the sparrow-hawk and especially the dung-beetle — Scarabaeus — Pl. 1 Fig. 2. Another symbol, frequently used, is the winged disk of the sun. Pl. 2 Fig. 2.

The capitals in Pl. 2 show also the application of the above mentioned vegetable motives, viz. Fig. 3 of the papyrus, Fig. 4 a capital composed of buds, the shaft representing a bundle of wood-stems, Fig. 5 palm-leaves and Fig. 6 a bud of the papyrus.

Fig. 1. Painted relief-figure from a column of the temple at Denderah.

„ 2 and 3. Paintings from mummy-cases.

„ 4 and 5. From a mummy-case in the Louvre, Paris.

„ 6. Painted border from a sarcophagus.

„ 7. Border from a mummy-case. British Museum, London.

„ 8. Ornament on a wooden sarcophagus. London.

„ 9. Border on a mummy-case. British Museum.

„ 10. Portion of a collar. London.

„ 11. Painting on a sarcophagus. London.

Plate 2.

EGYPTIAN.

ARCHITECTURE and PAINTING.

Fig. 1. Pylon (entrance-tower) with figural representations and hieroglyphics. Louvre, Paris.

„ 2. Cornice of the entablature of the great temple at Philae. Sculpture and painting.

„ 3. Capital from the temple at Luxor, representing full-blown papyrus. 1200 B. Chr.

„ 4. Capital from a temple at Thebes. (Buds-capital.)

„ 5. Capital from a portico at Edfu. (Representing a palm-tree.)

„ 6. Capital from Thebes, 1200 B. Chr. Represents a papyrus-bud.

„ 7. Mummy-case-painting.

„ 8 and 9. Scaly designs. Paintings from tomb-chambers. Louvre, Paris.

Printed by K. Hochdanz, Stuttgart, Germany.

PAINTING AND PLASTIC ART.

Printed by K. Hochdanz, Stuttgart, Germany.

ARCHITECTURE AND PAINTING.

Plate 3.

ASSYRIAN.

PAINTING. POLYCHROME SCULPTURE. POTTERY.

The excavations on the banks of the Tigris at Khorsabad, Nimroud and Koyunjik brought to light a great number of architectural remains, paintings and sculptures of Assyrian origin, which give us an idea of the magnificence and the exuberant luxury of the buildings of this nation. Assyrian ornament certainly betrays Egyptian influence, but there is no denying its originality. Besides geometrical figures, such as interlacements, zigzag lines, rosettes etc. animal and vegetable motives are used in sculpture and painting. Frequently we find even the so-called sacred tree (Fig. 11 and 12), mostly as bas-reliefs and painted, further winged griffins, lions and bulls with human faces. The winged male figure in the midst of our plate symbolizes the soul. For wall-coating glazed bricks frequently were employed and painted with regularly repeated figure-subjects or with interlacing designs.

Fig. 1. Portion of a glazed brick from a palace at Khorsabad.
  „ 2—4. Painted bas-reliefs from Koyunjik.
  „ 5. Painted ornament from Nimroud.
  „ 6. Glazed brick from Khorsabad.
  „ 7—10. Painted ornaments from Nimroud.
  „ 11—12. Sacred trees. Painted bas-reliefs from Nimroud.
  „ 13. Painted ornament from Nimroud.
  „ 14. Enamelled brick from Khorsabad.

Plate 4.

GREEK.

ORNAMENTAL ARCHITECTURE AND SCULPTURE.

Greek ornament preserves for ever a classical value, chiefly because the Grecian artists knew how to adapt the decoration to their artistic productions in such a way, that it nowhere overpowers the constructive groundwork, but rather accompanies it in beautiful lines and forms. Thus the fundamental form remains visible in its distinct substantiality, only relieved all the more by the ornament. Whether you look on the magnificent works of architecture or on the simplest objects for domestic use, produced by the Greeks, you will find, that all these works strike and surprise the beholder by their high perfection of form and their sublime beauty.

Fig. 1—3 show examples of the three forms of development of Greek architecture: of the Doric, Jonic and Corinthian styles.

The calm simplicity of the Doric capital expresses the purpose of supporting, and its forms put us in mind of the severity of the Doric race. Fig. 2 shows elegance and perfect grace, in conformity with the character of the Jonians. But in the exuberant forms of the Corinthian capital that love of splendour is represented, which from Corinth, the rich trading-place, spread over all Greece.

Fig. 4 shows one of those noble virginal figures, used instead of pillars in the Caryatide porch of the Erechtheium.

Fig. 1. Doric capital from Paestum (with painted ornaments).

„ 2. Jonic capital from the Erechtheium on the Acropolis of Athens.

„ 3. Corinthian capital from the Choragic Monument of Lysicrates at Athens.

„ 4. Caryatide from the Erechtheium.

„ 5 and 6. Acroteria from stelae (sepulchral columns), Paris.

„ 7—9. Anthemia-decorations.

„ 10 and 11. Griffins. Fragments of freezes.

„ 12 and 13. Legs of marble-tables in the National Museum at Naples.

„ 15 and 16. „ „ in the British Museum at London.

Printed by E. Hochdanz, Stuttgart. Germany.

PAINTING, POLYCHROME SCULPTURE, POTTERY.

ORNAMENTAL ARCHITECTURE AND SCULPTURE.

Plate 5.

GREEK.

POLYCHROME ARCHITECTURE.

––––––

Plate 5 shows a number of remains of polychrome (many-coloured) mouldings. These forms are in general the same conventional ones as we find in plastic ornament and likewise in the decorations of vases on Plate 6. (Meanders, heart-shaped leaves, ovolos, palmettes, anthemia-decorations etc.) It cannot now be questioned, that formerly colour was used in architecture; in fact, as the plastic ornaments were not seldom treated in a very flat way, they could hardly do without polychromy for producing an effect at long distances.

Fig. 1. Polychrome cyma (ogee) with lion's head from Selinus.
„ 2. Acroterium from the temple of Niké Apteros.
„ 3—6. Painted cornices from the Propylaea. Athens.
„ 7. Ornament of an antae-capital from the temple of Theseus. Athens.
„ 8. Ornament from a temple at Selinus.
„ 9. Frieze of the temple of Jupiter at Aegina.
„ 10. Cyma-ornament from the Parthenon.
„ 11. Ornament, found at Palazzolo.
„ 12 and 13. Meanders.
„ 14. Decoration of cassettes. London.
„ 15. Panel of metopes of baked clay, found at Palazzolo.
„ 16. Panel of cassettes from the Propylaea.

Plate 6.

GREEK.

POTTERY.

It was the Greeks, who raised pottery to a free art. Whereas in Egypt the labourers, a contempted caste, were charged with making the earthenware goods, which certainly were only used for domestic purposes or as a cheap substitute for precious vessels, the Greek potters, on the contrary, were so highly estimated that medals were stamped and monuments erected in their honour.

Vessels formed by hand, with plastic decorations, are very rare with the Greeks. The introduction of the potters wheel, already mentioned by Homer, took place in prehistoric times. Proofs of this kind of fabrication have also been found in the ruins of ancient Mycenae.

The oldest Greek vases are most simply decorated; on a light (white or yellowish) ground colour of clay brown bands, circles, squares etc. used to be painted. But soon they appear also with friezes, decorated with figures of animals.

Subsequently figural representations, treated after a scheme, appear between bands: undulating lines, heart-shapes and laurel-leaves, meanders etc. but, as before, dark on a light ground with frequent employment of white.

In the zenith of Greek ceramique art the colouring of the ground and of the ornamental and figural representations underwent a change. The orange colour of the clay was spared, the back ground filled with black. The figures, drawn with the brush, show much firmness and a noble elegance. Fig. 10.

Then followed a polychrome period which, without doubt, must be called the decay of Greek pottery. The colours now were used in larger masses, especially light-yellow, gold-yellow, blue, violet, even gold.

Fig. 1—9. Forms of Greek vases.
     „ 1. Amphora, vessel for oil, wine etc.
     „ 2. Hydria, vessel for carrying water.
     „ 3. Urn, a cinerary vessel.
     „ 4. Oenochoe, wine-can, pouring-vessel.
     „ 5. Cylix, drinking-cup.
     „ 6. Deinos, crater, vessel for mixing wine and water.
     „ 7. Lecythus, vessel for anointing-oil.
     „ 8. Cantharus, two-handled drinking-cup.
     „ 9. Rhyton, drinking-vessel.
Fig. 10. Female figure on an Amphora in the National Museum at Naples.
Fig. 11—32. Ornaments on vases in the Museums of Naples, Rome, Munich, Paris and London.

Printed by K. Hochdans, Stuttgart, Germany.

POLYCHROME ARCHITECTURE.

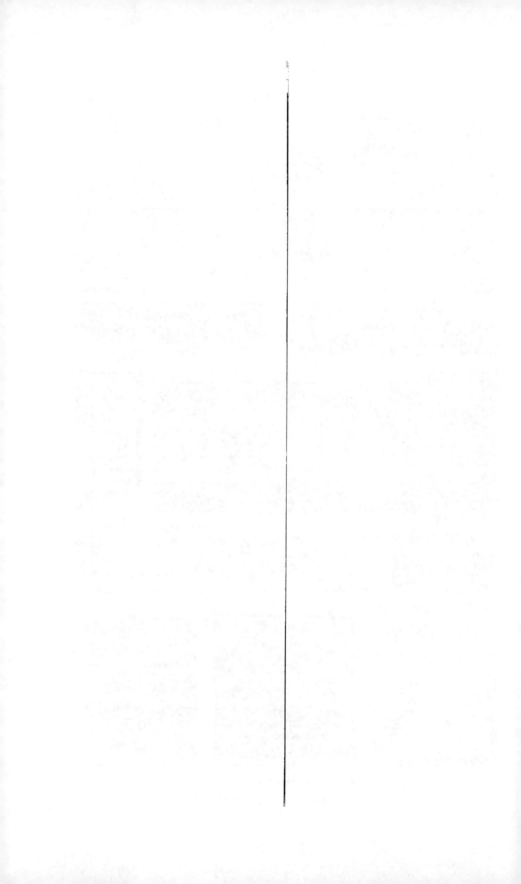

11. 12. 6. 2. 5. 1. 0. 4. 3. 7. 8. 13. 14.

15. 16. 17.

18. 19.

20. 21.

22. 23.

24. 25.

26. 10. 27.

28. 29.

30. 32. 31.

Printed by E. Hochdanz, Stuttgart, Germany.

POTTERY.

Plate 7.

ROMAN.

ORNAMENTAL ARCHITECTURE and SCULPTURE.

The Romans, for want of artistic talent of their own, seemed decidedly dependent on Etruscan, especially Grecian art; but instead of the classical pureness of forms we frequently meet here with an exaggerated decorative treatment.

In accordance with their love for pomp and splendour the Romans had a predilection for the Corinthian order, the capital of which they sometimes elaborated with very fine artistic feeling, for instance in the Pantheon at Rome, Fig. 1; whereas the form of the so-called Composite capital, Fig. 3, exhibits, on the contrary, a mechanical mixture of the Corinthian and Ionic styles. — An abundance of other Corinthian-like capitals, which we shall meet again in the Renaissance period, with dolphins, winged horses etc., in the place of volutes, prove the extravagant imagination of their inventors.

In Roman ornament the different forms of leaves often are idealised in such a rigid manner, that their natural origin is hardly to be recognized. Most frequently employed was the acanthus-leaf, but with its rounded points and fuller forms it appears much less fine and delicate than in Grecian art. Besides this we find oak-leaves, laurel, pine apples, vine-leaves, palm, ivy, aloe, convolvulus, cornear, poppy etc. alternately in bold execution, enlivened by a rich display of flowers, fruits and figural decorations.

Fig. 1. Corinthian capital from the Pantheon at Rome.

„   2. Head of a candelabrum from the Vatican Museum.

„   3. Composite capital from a temple of Juno at Rome.

„   4. Fragment of a frieze, found in the Villa of Hadrian at Tivoli, now in the Lateran Museum at Rome.

„   5 and 7. Rosettes from the Vatican Museum.

„   6. Fragment of a frieze from Rome.

„   8 and 11. Bases of columns from the later Roman period.

„   9 and 10. Members of cornices from the ruins of the Imperial palaces on the Palatine.

Plate 8.

ROMAN.

MOSAIC FLOORS.

———

Mosaic-work probably has its home in the East. This technical branch, considerably improved by the Greeks, was carried at last to the culminating point of perfection by the Romans, who produced not only geometrical mosaic-work, as we observe in so many floors excavated at Pompeii, but also flowers, animals, still-life, human and divine beings, even complete pictures, the latter being probably, for the most part, imitations of Greek originals no more existing.

Regarding the material, stones of different colours were generally employed, chiefly marble (seldom glass-pastes). In mosaic floors made of plates, Fig. 2 and 3, there is a great variety in the forms of the plates, whereas in mosaic proper, little stones, embedded in beton, were arranged into interesting carpet-patterns or figural representations, Fig. 1 and 4—10. Mosaics of this kind were also applied to walls and vaults.

In a later period motives like that on Plate 5, Fig. 13, with a tendency to relief-like appearance, were frequently used for floors, proving, that the taste of that period was already decaying.

— -   — ———————

Fig. 1. Mosaic frieze in the house of the Faun at Pompeii.

  „ 2 and 3. Patterns of plate-mosaic in the Palatine Museum at Rome (drawn by H. Dolmetsch)

  „ 4 and 5. Mosaic floors from the Hunting Villa at Fliessem near Trèves.

  „ 6 and 7. Mosaic floors from Pompeii (drawn by H. Dolmetsch).

  „ 8, 9 and 10. The same from the Thermae of Caracalla at Rome (drawn by H. Dolmetsch).

ORNAMENTAL ARCHITECTURE AND SCULPTURE.

Printed by Hoffmann, Stuttgart, Germany.

Printed by Max Seeger, Stuttgart, Germany.

MOSAIC FLOORS.

Plate 9.

POMPEIAN.

WALLPAINTING AND POLYCHROME BASSO-RELIEVOS.

The wallpaintings found at Pompeii, Herculaneum and Stabiae as well as at Rome, serving in the first place for decorative purposes only, can give us an idea of the lost Grecian painting; for probably most of them are reproductions of originals of Greek masters, although they are executed in a free-hand manner and impressed with the splendour-loving spirit of the Romans. — These pictures are usually painted al fresco in cheerful colours by mere artisans, but with admirable artistic feeling and bold mastership.

The apartments of the Pompeian houses are all without windows; the walls, being covered with lofty architectural designs, suggest the idea of increased size of the room. They are divided into a dado, a middle and an upper compartment The dado generally, has a black ground with simple ornaments or linear decorations; the purple, green, blue or yellow ground of the middle space is enlivened with one or more figures, landscapes etc., between pretty ornamental borders. The upper space is mostly white, enlivened with graceful scenes in various colours. There are, however, apartments, the walls of which begin with yellow dados and terminate with black friezes. Besides very rich arabesques, there are garlands, fruit, masks, candelabrums, animals, suspended arms etc. which, imitating nature with great fidelity, arrest the eyes of the beholder. — The most favourite plants were ivy and vine-branches, laurel, myrtle, cypress, olive and palm.

The walls always used to terminate at the top in a small painted stucco-cornice, from which the ceiling rose. The latter, frequently vaulted, was decorated with graceful variegated linear-ornaments on a light-coloured ground, or, often, with coloured stucco.

Fig. 1. Wallpainting, representing a figure of Victory, from Pompeii.

„ 2 and 3. Candelabrums, from the same place, in the Museum at Naples.

„ 4 and 5. Borders from Pompeii.

„ 6. Frieze at the same place (drawn by H. Dolmetsch).

„ 7 - 12. Borders from Herculaneum and Pompeii.

„ 13 and 14. Painted dados from Pompeii.

„ 15 - 20. Cornices, executed in stucco and painted, at the same place (drawn by H. Dolmetsch)

Plate 10.

POMPEIAN.

BRONZE.

The National Museum at Naples as well as the collections at Florence and other places in Italy afford a full survey of the smaller works of art and industry produced by the ancients. Contemplating the bronzes, down to the meanest objects for daily use, we are filled with high admiration for their noble and beautifully balanced shapes which interfere not at all with their practical usefulness.

There are candelabrums, lamps, little lamp-stands, most of them in tripod-form, vases, utensils for cooking, eating and drinking, in which the free and vigorous form of the profile, of the neck, but especially of the handles and ears was carried to great perfection; there are couches, coal-pans, theatrical masks, armatures and many other objects, all of which emit, as it were, the fresh breath of Grecian beauty, equally manifest in that wise moderation almost throughout observable.

The bronze statuettes are composed, as a rule, of several separately cast pieces, and many of them, on account of their highly artistic form, may fairly be reckoned among the best productions of the ancient world.

Fig. 1. Fountain-figure, representing a drunken Faun. One of the bronze figures, found at Pompeii (1880) and belonging to the most excellent works of this kind.

" 2 and 3. Two lamps (lucerna), in the Museum at Naples.

" 4 and 5. Great candelabrums, in the Collection of the Louvre at Paris.

" 6 and 8. „ „ in the Museum at Naples.

" 7. Side-view of the head of the candelabrum Fig. 6 (magnified).

" 9. Candelabrum-head, at Naples.

" 10. Two-armed small candelabrum with figure of a Faun, at Naples.

" 11. Bisellium, seat of honour for magistrates, beautifully profiled, in the Louvre at Paris.

" 12 and 13. Tripods from Herculaneum, in the Museum at Naples.

" 14 and 15. Little masks, being fragments of decorations, at Naples.

Printed by Max Seeger, Stuttgart, Germany.

WALLPAINTING AND POLYCHROME BASSO-RELIEVOS.

BRONZE.

Plate 12.

CHINESE.

PAINTING, WEAVING, EMBROIDERY and 'ÉMAIL CLOISONNÉ'.

The above mentioned fantastical mixture of patterns is characteristic of Chinese painting, although this peculiarity is somewhat covered by the great richness and successful combination of colours. In special favour are black, white, blue, red and gold outlines, by which the design is more prominently and beautifully relieved from the light or dark ground.

All we have said hitherto is likewise applicable in its full extent to Chinese silk-weaving and embroidery. It is well known that silk manufacture in China had reached a high degree of perfection long before the Christian era, but it may be less known that the gold-threads employed in Chinese weaving and embroidery most probably consisted of silk-threads covered with gilt-paper or caoutchouc-mass.

Most renowned, too, are the vases and dishes ornamented with so-called 'émail cloisonné'. Where this kind of enamelling was first invented, has up to now not been ascertained; the use of it by the Chinese is, however, of a very old date.

The process of making cloisonné work is as follows: — After the intended design has been traced upon the metal ground intended to be enamelled, the separate figures of the pattern are bordered by thin wire of gold or copper-alloy soldered to the metal-plate. The 'cloisons' so formed are then filled in with enamel of corresponding colour which is welded on in the furnace. When cool, the whole surface is polished smooth. Here too recur the same motives as in painting etc.

Fig. 10 shows, executed in this manner, the often-varied Imperial emblem of China, the primeval dragon (compare Fig. 6). According to a Chinese idea, man once developed out of the imperfect state of a dragon.

Fig. 1. Conventional representations of fruit and flowers painted on porcelain.

,, 2. Painted border from a China vessel.

,, 3. Painting from a little wooden chest.

,, 4, 5 and 6. Portions of bed-curtains embroidered in silk and gold (XV. century).

,, 7, 8 and 9. Patterns from woven stuffs.

,, 10 and 11. Portions of an old China copper-vase executed in 'émail cloisonné'.

,, 12 — 23. Ornaments on vases, bowls and censers executed in 'émail cloisonné'.

Printed by E. Hochdanz, Stuttgart, Germany.

PAINTING.

Printed by E. Hochdanz, Stuttgart, Germany.

PAINTING, WEAVING, EMBROIDERY AND ENAMEL.

Plate 13.

JAPAN.

LACKER-PAINTING.

Concerning the relation of Chinese to Japanese art compare the letterpress to Plate 14.

Of all productions of Japanese art, lacker-ware has attained a high and well-deserved celebrity long since; for this work shows an unrivalled technical perfection resulting from a traditional manufacture transmitted in the course of centuries from generation to generation within certain families. It is to the separation of the castes and guilds in Japan and China, that this more and more increasing perfection of artistic manufacture is to be ascribed.

Whereas the Chinese in ornamenting their lacker-ware employ, almost throughout, types from nature, the Japanese more frequently use geometrical or mere linear ornaments. But here as well as in other branches we often notice that apprehension of a systematical arrangement of the ornaments we have already mentioned when speaking of the Chinese. (Compare Fig. 1—8, 11, 12, 14, 20 and 21, 22 and 23; Plate 14, Fig. 10).

The style as well as the extremely complicated process of lacker-painting have remained unaltered up to now. The ground-material, consisting according to the intended purpose either of wood, layers of paper, papier-maché or plaited bast, after being smoothed on the surface by means of resin, is covered with as many coats of lacker, as the intended fineness of the articles requires. The most precious objects get sometimes as many as twenty such lacker-coatings and the necessary manipulations require a great deal of time and trouble. Sometimes mother-of-pearl or ivory is inlaid for decoration, but the most common practise is gilding, either by painting the gold afresh on the ornament with every new lacker-coat (hence an appearance of relief), or so, that the gilding, done but once, shines through the upper coat of the transparent lacker.

Lacker is supplied by nature as a ready product from the sap of a tree in different qualities, viz. yellow, brown and light yellow, the colour of the latter being soon changed in deep black with exposure to the air.

Fig. 1—50. Motives for lacker-painting.

Plate 14.

JAPAN.

WEAVING, PAINTING AND 'ÉMAIL CLOISONNÉ'.

It is hardly possible to point out exactly the characteristics which distinguish Chinese and Japanese productions of art from each other, an active commercial intercourse and an exchange of the successive acquirements and progress in industrial art having been kept up between both countries for ages, the result of this mutual teaching and learning being a uniformity of taste as well as of technical practises with both nations. That the latter reached a high point of perfection in these two countries, we have already remarked, but just in consequence of this utmost strain of technical skillfulness the intellectual element has been checked and the individual genius of the artists suppressed in China as well as, with some restriction, in Japan.

Although what we have said above in reference to the Plates 11 and 12 applies equally to Japanese art in general, it must be observed, that in our days, this art seems to revive with fresh vigor, excelling as it always did in a more regular style of ornamentation, in a closer observation of nature and a more individual freedom of design.

The Japanese got the advantage over the Chinese of applying cloisonné work, as a novelty, to porcelain vases. In this technical manipulation, (never yet succeeded in by Europeans,) the metal wires are fixed on the objects by means of enamel of high fusibility, after the glaze has been removed from the parts concerned. The further proceeding is the same as we have described with Plate 12.

It is a remarkable fact, that, although the Chinese had taught the Japanese porcelain-manufacture, yet the latter nation was early renowned for having far surpassed its masters, not only in quality and fineness of its productions, but also in regard of their enormous size. This superiority applies to painted dishes and vases as well as to those colossal articles, which, being covered all over with 'émail cloisonné', exhibit in their deep and sad colouring a wonderful magnificence and harmony.

Fig. 1—7. Borders and patterns from silk stuffs.
„ 8 and 9. Paintings from an old porcelain-vase.
„ 10. Painting from an old cup-shaped vase.
„ 11 and 12. Borders from two fayence-vases.
„ 13—19. Ornaments from enamelled vases (16, 17 and 19 are modern).

LACKER-PAINTING

WEAVING, PAINTING AND ENAMEL.

Plate 15.

INDIAN.

METAL WORK.

Compare also the letterpress to Plate 16.

The manufacture of decorated arms and metal ware was at all times an important branch of the Indian industrial art, and we have due cause to be astonished at the refinement of taste combined with the highest magnificence of ornamentation.

Damascene work, specially exemplified on our plate, is executed in steel, iron or tin-alloy, in the latter case the design being brought out in deep black by the agency of sulphur.

The damascened ornaments are made in silver- and gold-foil, fixed on either by pressure or hammering to the metal ground, which has previously been slightly engraved, after which the whole is polished with the burnisher.

Fig. 1. Tin-vessel with damascened ornaments.

„ 2. Battle-axe with etched decorations.

„ 3. Battle-axe with damascene work.

„ 4. Shield of rhinoceros-skin inlaid and mounted with metal. .

„ 5—8. Ornaments from damascened Huhkas (water-pipes).

„ 9. Belly-decoration, executed "en repoussé", of a gilt copper-can.

„ 10. Belly-decoration from a copper-can in repoussé work.

„ 11. Decoration from a damascened tin-vase.

„ 12. Damascene work on steel on a dagger-sheath.

„ 13. Neck-decoration on a damascened tin-cup.

„ 14. From a copper-plate in repoussé work.

„ 15. From a tin-plate in repoussé work.

Fig. 2, 9, 10, 12—15 drawn after original objects from the Royal "Landesgewerbemuseum" at Stuttgart.

„ 1. 5—8 and 11 drawn after original objects belonging to Mr. Paul Stotz, manufacturer at Stuttgart.

Plate 16.

INDIAN.

EMBROIDERY, WEAVING, PLAITING AND LACQUERWORK.

I ndia, that country full of luxurious vegetation, rich in natural products of every kind, with inexhaustible mines of precious metals and stones, displays her character of overflowing abundance and the fantastic spirit of her inhabitants also in the productions of her art. But notwithstanding her old and comparatively high civilisation, a certain conservatism, extending for nearly a thousand years to the social and religious conditions and institutions, exercised, as a matter of course, its unavoidable influence also on the artistic productions, especially when you look on the caste-like separation of the several trades. Only since the beginning of our century can we report new introductions in the Indian art.

Being little conventional and flowing freely, Indian ornament seems to have the greatest affinity with the Persian style. The surface decoration, never losing its specific character, mostly exhibits a very profuse richness of recurring motives, and a grand splendour of colouring which, far from harassing the eyes of the beholder, affords, on the contrary, a salutary repose to them. The outlines of the design, in which all modelling is avoided, are generally executed on light ground in deeper colours than the pattern itself, and on dark ground in light colours. The Indians found their principal motives, as seems most likely, among their native plants, employing in the first place lotus, excellently drawn roses, pinks, granates, etc.; but most frequently, especially in modern productions, we meet with the palm-branch always treated conventionally (Fig. 11 and Plate 15, Fig. 9, 15; Plate 17, Fig. 23, 28 and 29).

In consequence of British competition, the art of weaving, formerly brought to the highest perfection, s now decaying; also in modern silk embroidery the former quiet harmony is frequently disturbed by using the too vivid aniline colours. But the Cashmere shawls, being celebrated for ages all over the world, will still keep their renown for a long time owing to their unrivalled fineness and delicacy and to their magnificent colours. Many-coloured cotton carpets (Fig. 8. and 9), the striped design of which is excellently fitted to the stuff, are widely spread as a cheap substitute for woolen carpets. — The plaited mats too are well worthy of our attention, as regards their colour and design (Fig. 10.)

Indian lacquerwork, when compared with the Chinese and Japanese, is somewhat less finished, as regards technical perfection, and it differs from them in this essential point, that the lacquer serves only, as it were, to preserve the gilt or polychrome ornaments.

Fig. 1. Embroidered carpet of the 16th century.
  „ 2—6. Borders from silk-embroideries.
  „ 7. Pattern embroidered in silk.
  „ 8 and 9. Cotton carpets.
  „ 10. Mat of plaited rushes.
  „ 11 and 12. Border patterns of Cashmere shawls.
  „ 13. Painted lacquerwork.

Printed by E. Hochdanz, Stuttgart, Germany.

METAL WORK.

EMBROIDERY, WEAVING, PLAITING AND LACKERWORK.

Table 16 A.

INDIAN.

INLAYS IN MARBLE.

If we cast a glance at old Indian Architecture, we are at once struck by the unmistakeable character of an exceedingly varied and complex style, which however may very likely be traced back to ages long gone by. Even the most ancient monuments of India consisted of stucco-work richly embellished with sculpture, mosaics and colors whose technics naturally favored the display of a pompous richness. This same over-loading was later on extended also to rock-and quarry-stone buildings and thus the places of worship as well as the Palaces of India present a bewildering diversity and phantastical oddities. A hundredfold repetition of idol's pictures or long rows of lions and elephants, phantastic and colossal figures of men supporting, caryatide-like, the projecting cornices, all sorts of mythological representations, descriptions of battles and victories with a motley crowd of inscriptions between.

The characteristics on the forms of the columns, pillars and pilasters which are worked out with infinite variation, are the continually recurring change from the angular to the circular form, the frequent cording with narrow bands and the bulging out of the capitals. On these latter arises, console-like, a broadly projecting flag-stone, resembling a wooden structure, which very often supports a reposing lion, the symbol of Buddha. (See table 15, fig. 16 and table 16 fig. 15.) In later periods, after Arabian influence had introduced the Mahommedan style also into India, a peculiar grandeur became observable on the buildings and this, with the help of curved and pointed arches forming arcades as also the introduction of mighty cupolas presents internally and externally a new feature, which frequently culminates in a truly extravagant splendor. This period had its climax in the XVI and the first half of the XVIII century. It is to the first-named epoch that the marble-marquetries from the Mogul tombs at Agra belong, which are sketched on the table above-referred to. These artistically furnished mausoleums were built with white marble, whilst all prominent architectural parts of the structure were ornamented with manifold colored stones, such as jasper, heliotrope, chalcedony, agate etc. Every curved line, every closed bud and opening flower we find represented with a sweet regard to the beauties of nature and besides this all is in thorough harmony with those venerable mosaic technics.

Fig. 10.

Fig. 1 to 9.   Marble marquetry from the mausoleums af the Shah Jehán
and the Begum Mumtáz-i-Mahal.
„   10. Filigree Panel of red sandstone, at Fathepore-Sikri.

Taken from „Portfolio of Indian Art and the Journal of Indian Art."

INLAYS IN MARBLE.

Plate 17.

INDIAN.

METAL WORK, EMBROIDERY, WEAVING and PAINTING.

A rtistically employed, especially in goldsmiths' work, was the so-called "émail champlevé". The parts intended to be enamelled on the metal, were deepened with the burin, narrow rims being left to separate the several compartments. The further process is nearly the same as we have described when speaking of "émail cloisonné". — A brilliant specimen of that work may be seen in Fig. 4, representing an ancus (instrument used to drive and train elephants).

We often meet with illumination in India, betraying however Persian influence and applied to old royal edicts, documents and other manuscripts of religious and poetical contents.

Fig. 1. Ancus in chiselled iron.

  „ 2 and 3. Pendants and button embossed in gold and chiselled.

  „ 4. Ancus, enamelled and adorned with jewels.

  „ 5—9. Decorations from enamelled arms.

  „ 10. State parasol with rich gold embroidery.

  „ 11—13. Embroidered fans.

  „ 14. Covering for the foot, woven in gold and embroidered in silk and pearls.

  „ 15. Embroidered table-cover.

  „ 16. Border from a saddle-cloth.

  „ 17. Embroidery on black stuff.

  „ 18. Border from an embroidered velvet-carpet.

  „ 19—22. Flowers from silk embroidery.

  „ 23. Woven shawl.

  „ 24. Border from woven stuff.

  „ 25 and 26. Patterns from silk- and gold-weavings.

  „ 27. Lacquerpainting.

  „ 28. Portion of a book-cover in lacquerpainting.

  „ 29 and 30. From illuminated manuscripts.

Plate 18.

PERSIAN.

ARCHITECTURE.

A great number of monumental buildings, although more or less dilapidated, conveys to the present day an idea of the fairy-like magnificence of the ancient empire of the Caliphs, as well as of the gorgeous palaces and mosques of Persia. Especially in Ispahan, her former capital, a series of examples still proves how well the Persians understood to give a rich appearance to their edifices by employing glazed tiles, either variegated or painted. Almost all the domes of the mosques, chiefly pear or bulb-shaped, and the points of the minarets, as well as their walls and, in short, nearly all parts of these buildings are covered with such tiles. (Fig. 1, 6, 7, 10, 11.)

This rich polychrome ornamentation, so abundantly used, is not less characteristic of the Persian architecture, when compared with any other Mohamedan, than the peculiar mode of decoration. The latter shows much less variety in combining geometrical ornaments (Fig. 11), than we find with the Arabs and Moors, and in the floral ornament, though conventionally treated, there still prevails an attempt at the imitation of nature, the rich vegetation of the country offering a great variety of subjects. Scroll-work and flowers are either separately distributed over the surfaces, or interspersed between the linear ornaments.

An interesting feature is the frequently occurring pierced stone window-frames, the open spaces being filled in with painted glass (Fig. 8 and 15).

We may mention here, also as worthy of notice, the so-called stalactite vaults (Fig. 14) composed of small vaultings projecting one above the other.

Fig. 1. Upper part of a minaret from the mosque Mesdjid-i-Chah.

  „ 2—5. Bases and capitals of columns.

  „ 6. Wall-border from the portal building of the mosque Mesdjid-i-Chah.

  „ 7. Decorated cavetto from the same.

  „ 8. Pierced stone window-frame (belonging to Fig. 12).

  „ 9. Wall-border.

  „ 10 and 11. Spandrels from the College Medresseh-Maderi-Chah-Sultan-Hussein.

  „ 12. Pierced stone window-arch (the dotted ground means stained glass).

  „ 13. Entablature from the Pavillon Tchehel-Soutoun.

  „ 14. Stalactite vault from the Pavilion of the eight Paradise-gates.

  „ 15—17. Divers dome-points.

The whole from Ispahan.

Printed by K. Hochdanz, Stuttgart, Germany.

METAL WORK, EMBROIDERY, WEAVING AND PAINTING.

Printed by Hoffmann Stuttgart, Germany.

ARCHITECTURE.

Plate 19.

PERSIAN.

POTTERY.

The beautiful fayence ware produced by Persian industry was at all times a considerable article of export. In all countries professing Islam the productions of this very early and highly developed industry are found 'down to the present time.

After having remarked with regard to Plate 18, the dazzling manner in which the Persians decorated the exterior of their buildings with tiles, we must especially record here their tastefully coloured dishes, of which Plate 19 gives some examples.

Both the invariably flat treatment of the ornament and the prevalence of the natural imitation of flowers constitute the characteristic style of Persian decoration.

Fig. 1—5. Ancient Persian fayence plates in the Musée Cluny at Paris.
  „ 6 and 7. Borders from walls wainscoted with fayence.

Fig. 3. After an original drawing bei C. Bauer from the "Kunstbibliothek der Kgl. Centralstelle für Gewerbe und Handel" at Stuttgart.

Plate 20.

PERSIAN.

WEAVING AND ILLUMINATION.

In pottery as well as in weaving and illumination, we find the use of secondary and tertiary colours predominating, which being mostly in complete harmony with each other and the ground colour, produce a certain delicacy and brightness of coloration, which distinguishes all those objects.

Owing to these circumstances the Persian carpets covered with flowers and in many cases enlivened with animals and birds, and the delicately painted Koran-manuscripts are widely dispersed and much in favour throughout the East. But on account of the masses being rather unevenly distributed over the surfaces, the productions of Persian art are considered somewhat inferior to those of the Arabs and Moors.

In Fig. 1. we see almost all flowers conventionally treated, and in Fig. 3. the large leaves idealised in a manner quite usual with the Arabs (compare also Plate 19, Fig. 1.).

Fig. 1. Persian carpet, 16th century.

„ 2. Motives for weaving from an old Persian book of ornaments in the Museum of Ornamental Art at London.

„ 3. Illumination from a Koran.

Printed by K. Hochdanz, Stuttgart, Germany.

POTTERY.

Printed by E. Hochdanz, Stuttgart, Germany.

WEAVING AND ILLUMINATION.

Plate 21.

PERSIAN.

METAL WORK.

In all ages weapons, armature and metal vessels of Persian origin were highly estimated in the East as well as in Western countries up to the present day. Being decorated with excellent Damascene work or beautifully embossed, they exhibit in their ornaments the above-described features of the Persian style in perpetual variation. Moreover we are struck by Persian characters expressing proverbs or religious sentences (Fig. 1 and 2 and Plate 18, Fig. 1). Animals and human figures are likewise represented in sometimes fantastical imitations (Fig. 1, 2 and 8).

Fig. 1 and 2. Helm with shield belonging to it.

„ 3. Border from an armature.

„ 4 — 8. Decorations on metal vessels.

„ 9— 12. Portions of eating-utensils.

Fig. 1—8 drawn after original objects from the Royal 'Landesgewerbemuseum' at Stuttgart.

Plate 22.

PERSIAN-ARABIAN.

WAINSCOT IN GLAZED CLAY.

Our Plate represents a wainscot of the XVI. century in the mosque of Ibrahim Aga at Cairo, exemplifying a mixture of the Persian and Arabian styles, inasmuch as the predominance of vegetable ornamentation directly points at Persian influence.

Printed by Max Seeger, Stuttgart, Germany.

METAL WORK.

Printed by Max Seeger, Stuttgart, Germany.

WAINSCOT IN GLAZED CLAY.

Plate 23.

ARABIAN.

WEAVING, EMBROIDERY AND PAINTING.

———

Hardly 250 years had elapsed since the establishment of Islam through Mahomet, when the Arabs had already developed a style of their own, which, though frequently following Persian, Roman and Byzantine examples, yet possesses its peculiar features. This is especially the case in their style of decoration, which perfectly demonstrates their artistic talent being identical with their nature and feeling.

A simple imitation of real beings could not be in accordance either with their boundless lavish imagination or with their character, imbued with poetry; representations of men or animals are therefore of comparatively rare occurrence, although images are not actually forbidden by the Koran, as is pretended. The Arabian artists, however, found full satisfaction in that pompous ornamentation which, most extensively employed in all branches of their artistic performances, engages both the eye and the intellect. They created in changeful play an abundance of rich combinations of lines, called Arabesques after their inventors, the Arabs, consisting either of figures geometrically constructed or of foliage rigidly idealised. In such intertwisted scroll work, exhibiting its finest forms in ingenious rosettes and stars, the principle prevails, that each scroll and each leaf is always traceable to its root and parent stem. Brilliant colours serve more especially to disentangle the seemingly insoluble intricacy, and to diffuse a quiet harmony over the decorated surface.

The curved points of the leaves are a specific characteristic of such Arabian foliage (Fig. 3).

The Arabs seem also to have first introduced those ingenious patterns, of which we see a specimen in the midst of Fig. 2, where two similar figures, lying in an opposite direction, are produced by one single line.

Finally the upper part of Fig. 1 may serve as an example of the ornamental adaptation of writing, as it was not at all rare with the Arabs.

———

Fig. 1. Woven carpet of the XIV. century, preserved in the church at Nivelles.

„ 2. Embroidered Appliqué work of the XVIII. century.

„ 3. A portion of the richly painted ceiling of the mosque el Bordeyny at Cairo.

Plate 24.

ARABIAN.

ORNAMENTS IN WOOD AND METAL.

To prevent looking in from the outside without hindering a free look-out, the window-openings facing the street were furnished with wooden lattices, shaped by art in a very elegant manner (Fig. 2 and 3). Especially, however, the inventive ingenuity of Arabian art-workmen was engaged in decorating the doors.

Fig. 1 for instance presents us a panel of a richly carved and chiselled door, whilst in Fig. 5—15 a great selection of bronze door fittings will be found, the latter being applied so as either to form the ornament itself, or so that the parts of the wood uncovered by the metal, bring out the pattern. Fig. 4 is an escutcheon executed in bronze, and occurring also on many Arabian coins.

Printed by K. Hochdanz, Stuttgart, Germany.

WEAVING, EMBROIDERY AND PAINTING.

ORNAMENTS IN WOOD AND METAL.

Plate 25.

ARABIAN.

ILLUMINATION OF MANUSCRIPTS.

Likewise in their paintings on parchment the Arabian artists show special skill in surface decoration. Scroll work, rigidly idealised, alternates with geometrical figures, or else the arabesque ornament fills the compartments formed by the lines and bands. In this manner whole pages are painted in many Koran manuscripts, from which Fig. 4 and 5 give us four specimens of coloured motives of this rich mode of treatment. — The writing itself is in most cases bordered and surrounded with rosettes and freezes, which are filled in with ever new combinations of lines and foliage.

The splendid and at the same time harmonious effect of this illumination arises principally from the exquisite arrangement of the colours, the brilliancy of which is still enhanced by a profuse employment of gold.

A glance at Fig. 6 with its many-coloured flowers might induce us to suppose Persian or Indian influence, and Romanesque in Fig. 8 and 9; everywhere, however, we see the curved or involuted points of the leaves which characterize the art of the Arabs and Moors.

Fig. 1. Decoration from an Arabian Koran   XIV. century.

   „ 2 and 3. Decorations from an Arabian Koran   XVI.   „

   „ 4 and 5.   „   „   a Moorish   „   XVIII.   „

   „ 6 and 7.   „   „   an Arabian   „   XVI.   „

   „ 8—10.   „   „   „   „   „   XVII.   „

   „ 11 and 12.   „   „   a Moorish   „   XVIII.   „

Plate 26.

ARABIAN-MORESQUE.

ARCHITECTONIC ORNAMENTS.

Arabian and Moorish architecture is of importance for us on account of some of their mouldings being entirely covered with ornaments, sometimes magnificently gilded and painted. Freezes and cornices received their particular adornment by pinnacles, either simply and plainly treated (Fig. 11 and 12), or richly decorated (Fig. 13—15).

The columns at first followed Egyptian and Byzantine examples or were, in fact, composed of parts of Greek or Roman columns; later on however (since about the 12th. century) they were formed in a style of their own, the capital consisting mainly of a cube decorated with foliage and scroll work (Fig. 6 and Plate 28, Fig. 1).

A most artistic treatment is exhibited especially in vaults and portions of vaults composed of more or less gorgeous stalactites.

Fig. 1 represents a wall decoration executed in plaster and low-relief and in many cases coloured. Here we meet the so-called Arabian feather, so very frequently employed, especially in the Alhambra (compare Fig. 13; Plate 24, Fig. 4, 7, 11; Plate 28, Fig. 2, 6, 7, 9, 10).

Fig. 1. Panel from the Alhambra.
   „   2. Decoration in stone above a door in Cairo.
   „   3 and 4. Base and capital of a column from Cairo.
   „   5. and 6. „ „   „   „ „   „   „   the Alhambra.
   „   7 and 8. Stalactites from Cairo.
   „   9 and 10. Corbels from Cairo.
   „   11—15. Pinnacles from Cairo.

Printed by E. Hochdanz, Stuttgart, Germany.

ILLUMINATION OF MANUSCRIPTS.

ARCHITECTONIC ORNAMENTS.

Plate 27.

ARABIAN-MORESQUE.

MOSAIC WORK and GLAZED CLAY WORK.

Arabian and Moorish mosaics are made partly of small pieces of coloured marble, partly of small clay plates, painted and glazed. Sometimes (as in Fig. 5—11) the designs are cut into the marble plates and the deepenings filled in with coloured cement.

In these mosaics the geometrical principle predominates. Regarding the colours used, it is noticeable that the secondary and tertiary colours were most in favour; it may also be observed, that the Moors, relinquishing here the primary colours exclusively used by them at other times, preferred on the contrary green and orange.

These mosaics served for covering the floors as well as the lower parts of the walls.

Fig. 1, 3 and 4. Wainscottings of glazed clay from the Alhambra.
„ 2. Wainscotting of glazed clay from the mosque of the Cheykhoun at Cairo.
„ 5—7 and 9—11. Marble wainscottings inlaid with stucco from Cairo.
„ 8, „ „ „ „ „ „ Damascus.

Plate 28.

MORESQUE.

ARCHITECTONIC ORNAMENTS.

Spain is the country, where the Islamitic art found its purest and most beautiful development in the buildings of the Moorish kings, for instance, in the palace of Alhambra near Granada (13th and 14th century). Especially with the Moors, Mahomedan ornamentation reached its culminating point.

Fig. 2—10 represent mouldings and wall surfaces executed in stucco and painted. The characteristics of Arabian ornamentation, hitherto mentioned, are identical with Moorish, but it may be added, that the former is neither so happy in the distribution of the ornament over the surface, nor so varied as the latter. The Moorish artists knew how to produce wonderful effects by artfully interlacing and twisting the geometrical and arabesque ornaments; for here they could give full play, so to speak, to their richly gifted imagination. Therefore, we find two (Fig. 6, 7, 9) and sometimes even three systems of ornaments (Fig. 10) worked into each other, and this richness is still increased by the bands and leaves being covered with fine ornaments. This profusion, however, is far from troubling and disquieting the eye, for design and colour being perfectly appropriate to disconnect the single systems, each of them can be very well distinguished from the other, whereas all together effect a splendid harmony, and surprise the attentive beholder again and again with new beauties. The ornament, executed always in very low relief, never loses its character as surface decoration.

The prominent bands and scrolls in most cases are gilt; when the ground is red, the feather decorations of the leaves are blue, or the reverse; sometimes red and blue change alternately in the ground Besides these three primary colours, white is frequently employed.

That writing too very frequently served as ornamentation, is to be seen in Fig. 6, 7 and 10.

Our 10 illustrations have been taken exclusively from the Alhambra.

Printed by K. Hochdanz, Stuttgart, Germany.

MOSAIC WORK AND GLAZED CLAY WORK.

Printed by K. Hochdanz, Stuttgart, Germany.

ARCHITECTONIC ORNAMENTS.

Plate 29.

TURKISH.

ARCHITECTONIC ORNAMENTS IN GLAZED CLAY.

We can hardly speak of a proper style indicating the genius of the Turkish nation before the 15th century. Previous to that for instance the Christian churches of the conquered countries were either changed into mosques, or Christian artists were charged with the erection of new buildings. Likewise the art of ornamentation was essentially influenced first by Byzantine, and later on by Persian and Arabian modes of decoration. Finally from a mixture of the two latter styles Turkish ornamentation took its origin.

What strikes us here first of all, is the frequent recurrence in leaves and scrolls of the re-entering angle, which has its origin in Persia (compare Plate 20, Fig. 3); next we observe a certain poverty of the scroll work, which (especially when compared with Moorish treatment) leaves large spaces of the ground free and uncovered (Fig. 5, 6). Moreover the decorations painted on the leaves with different colours, are frequently wanting in form, whereas the Turkish artist also likes ingenious interlacements of several systems of lines. — The colours used, are not very brilliant, and looking at their combination, we miss the splendour and abundance of Arabian and Moorish art. In earlier times the ground nearly always had a deep sad blue, whereas in later works green or light red predominate.

Fig. 8, 10, 11 furnish proof, that in the ornament of the Islamitic nations, the Persian floral element always bursts forth afresh and in comparative pureness. Altogether it is to be noted, that numerous productions of Persian art, especially painted clay plates etc., were imported and used by the Turks.

Fig. 1, 2 5, 6, 7 and 9. From the Mosque of Yéchil-Djami at Brussa.

„ 3, 4 and 8. From the Yéchil-Turbey-Tomb of Sultan Mohammed I.

„ 10 and 11. From the Tomb Mourahdieh.

Plate 30.

CELTIC.

ILLUMINATION OF MANUSCRIPTS.

———

Among the Celtic population of Ireland there was already in very early times an original style of orna-ment developed, the commencement of which no doubt goes far back to the days when heathenism still prevailed in that island. To this period may be ascribed the origin of several stone coffins, which show the same decorations as we find in the manuscripts of Celtic monks down from the 6th century. This ornamentation, not at all influenced by Byzantine or some other south- or east-European art, bears a cha-racter of its own, for the relics of it, found also with the Scandinavian nations, are certainly traceable to Ireland.

In the eldest Celtic or Irish manuscripts the large initial letters were at first distinguished by a network of red dots surrounding them (compare Fig. 1, lower part). Soon afterwards however, the artists proceeded to the proper interlaced ribbon work, in the employment of which they exhibit a surprising skilfulness and variety (Fig. 1, 3, 9). With similar work, frequently used as decoration, we meet again in the Renaissance period.

For Celtic interlacing work, either filling up the spare surfaces of the letters or bordering the separate pages, the limbs or bodies of snakes, birds, dogs and fantastical animals were employed (Fig. 1, 5, 9). Occasionally the human figure occurs, whereas the vegetable ornament is wholly wanting. Its introduction first dates from the 9th century, and after weak commencements (compare Fig. 8) it spreads more and more, next the ribbon ornament, under the influence of the Romanesque style.

The number of colours is a small one, in the beginning especially, gold occurs only in a later epoch.

———

Fig. 1—5.   From the VII. century.
  „ 6 and 7.   „   „ VIII.   „
  „ 8.   „   „ IX.   „
  „ 9—11.   „   „ X.   „
  „ 12.   „   „ XI.   „

Printed by K. Hochdanz, Stuttgart, Germany.

ARCHITECTONIC ORNAMENTS IN GLAZED CLAY.

ILLUMINATION OF MANUSCRIPTS.

Plate 32.

BYZANTINE.

INCRUSTED ENAMEL, MARBLE-MOSAIC
AND GLASS-MOSAIC.

I ncrusted enamel was not less cultivated than "cloisonné work". Fig. 1 shows us, executed in this manner, Christ enthroned on a rainbow and surrounded by the symbols of the four Evangelists. This figure proves that in course of time, a certain lifelessness prevailed in the figural representations; specially looking on the image in the middle, we are struck by the expression of quietness having quite grown into rigidity.

In marble mosaic, with which the floors were lavishly covered, decorative art again made use of the various changes of geometrical motives. In this practice the Byzantine artists have given many ideas to the Mohammedan. However a conventional treatment of foliage and scroll work is not excluded and reminds us, as mentioned, of antique examples.

Fig. 1. Book-cover of gilt bronze decorated with incrusted enamel and stones, XII. century, in the Museo Correi at Venice.

„ 2, 3 and 5. Marble mosaics from floors in S. Alessio at Rome.

„ 4. Marble mosaics from floors in S. Maria in Cosmedin ibid.

„ 6. „ „ „ „ „ S. Vitale at Ravenna.

„ 7. Glass mosaics from S. Maria in Araceli at Rome.

„ 8. „ „ „ S. Alessio at Rome.

„ 9 and 10 Glass mosaics from the Duomo at Messina.

„ 11—13. „ „ „ „ „ „ Monreale.

„ 14—16. „ „ „ „ Facade of the Cathedral of Orvieto.

„ 17 and 18. Marble-mosaic-bands from capitals in St. Mark's at Venice.

„ 19 and 20. „ „ „ from the walls of Sta. Sofia, Constantinople.

Fig. 1. After an original drawing by A. Borkhardt, architect at Stuttgart.
„ 2—5, 7, 8, 14, 15 and 16 after original drawings by H. Dolmetsch at Stuttgart.

Printed by F. Hochdanz, Stuttgart, Germany.

GLASS-MOSAIC, COLOURED ENAMEL AND ILLUMINATION.

Printed by E. Hochdanz, Stuttgart, Germany.

INCRUSTED ENAMEL, MARBLE-MOSAIC AND GLASS-MOSAIC.

Plate 33.

BYZANTINE.

WEAVING AND EMBROIDERY.

Even since the importation of silk in the 6th century, Byzantium could succesfully compete in woven fabrics with the Asiatic productions of this class, taking the lead in Europe till far into the 12th century. During this period an extensive trade was carried on in the most precious woven fabrics, figured or not, in gorgeous embroidered materials and stuffs, adorned beads (Fig. 3, 5, 7 and 8). The Sarazene weavers in the island of Sicily rivaled, it is true, the Byzantine; however it was not before the conquest of Sicily by the Normans, when a great number of captive Grecian weavers were transported to Palermo, (thus uniting Christian and Mohamedan art), that the stuffs and robes from the Royal manufactures of Sicily attained the highest value in the emporiums of the world for their splendour and their beautiful designs.

Plate 33 shows us such Sicilian articles exhibiting clearly the influence of Arabian ornamentation, without denying Byzantine forms. — In these woven fabrics the ornament is always treated as surface decoration. The plants and animals which we see applied, do not exactly imitate nature, but are more or less idealised. — In Fig. 9 the lion overpowering the camel seems intended to symbolize Christianity overruling Islam.

Fig. 1. Embroidered purple robe in the cathedral-treasure at Bamberg.

„   2. Figured silk-stuff on the tunic of Henry II. in the National-Museum at Munich.

„   3, 4 and 7. Embroidered borders from the Imperial Alb in the Imp. treasury at Vienna.

„   5 and 6. Embroidered borders from the Imperial tunicle ibid.

„   8. Embroidered borders on the German Emperor's mantle in the Imperial treasury at Vienna.

„   9. Embroidery on the German Emperor's mantle ibid.

„   10 and 11. Patterns painted on garments from tomb-stones in the church S. Lorenzo Fuori le mura at Rome.

Plate 34.

BYZANTINE AND MIDDLE-AGES.

ARCHITECTURE AND SCULPTURE.

Although on the whole the difference between Byzantine and Romanesque architecture is very considerable (when we look on both styles in general), yet as regards decorative details, it moves within very narrow limits, which fact is easily accountable from the above mentioned active export of Byzantine objects of art into Western countries, and from the influence of Byzantine artists.

The Byzantine capital is either an imitation of antique capitals, especially of the Corinthian (Fig. 1), or it exhibits an original shape in the form of a cube contracted at the bottom, and rounded off at its lower angles (Fig. 2). In the former case however, the treatment of the foliage, inclining with its broad indentments and sharp points to a certain rigidness, does no longer manifest that close observation of nature, as in the classical period. In the latter case the four sides are framed with low raised ribbon or plaited work inclosing either foliage, always conventionally treated, or symbolical figures.

Romanesque architecture shaped its capitals either in Corinthian-like or Byzantine-like manner (cushion capital), or it created special forms in its bell-shaped and calyculate capitals, these being either plainly treated or richly ornamented. Most frequently we find the cushion capitals covered with figural ornaments (Fig. 10), human figures and animals, often fantastically transformed, not being generally, despised as means of decoration. Besides these, the so-called tarin-capitals were frequently used. — As decoration for pillar-shafts, key-stones, friezes, cornices etc., scroll work and foliage were in great favour, appearing, without exception, in idealised forms, and often showing, at least in the first times, an inferior understanding of nature. The leaves are broadly treated and their points frequently rounded. — To produce an effective change of light and shadow, all forms were worked out in very high relief, sometimes almost completely standing out from the ground, as in Fig. 13. — Fig. 13 and 14 belong already to the so-called transition-style.

Fig.　1. Capital from Agia Theotokos at Constantinople. Close of IX. century.
　　　2. Capital from S. Vitale at Ravenna.
　　　3. Lintel-decoration from Agia Theotokos at Constantinople.
　　　4. Chaptrel-cornice from the church of St. Nicolas at Myra.
　　　5. Pilaster-capital from Agia Sofia at Constantinople.
　　　6. Door-frame on the abbey-church at St. Denis. Midst of XII. century.
　　　7. Panel.
　　　8. Pillar-decoration from the cathedral at Bourges.
　　　9.　„　„　„　„　„　„　„
　　10. Capital from the abbey-church at St. Benoit.
　　11.　„　„　„　Barbarossa-palace at Gelnhausen.
　　12. Arch-border from the church St. Amant de Boixe.
　　13.　„　„　„　„　„　at Gelnhausen. Beginning of the XIII. century.
　　14. Console　„　„　„　„　„　„　„　„　„　„
　　15. Decoration of a pillar-shaft from the church at Tournus XII. century.
　　16.　„　„　„　„　„　„　„　„　„　„　„　cathedral at Chartres.
　　17. From a door-frame from the former Benedictine-abbey-church at Ellwangen.
　　18. Frieze in the interior of St. Walderich's chapel at Murrhardt.
　　19 and 20. Arch-consols on the side-aisle of St. Sebald, Nuremberg.
　　21. Key-stone-decoration in the same church.
　　22.　„　„　„　from the cathedral at Bamberg.

Printed by E. Hochdanz, Stuttgart, Germany.

WEAVING AND EMBROIDERY.

Printed by Hoffmann, Stuttgart, Germany.

ARCHITECTURE AND SCULPTURE.

RUSSIAN.

MANUSCRIPT-PAINTING.

The old slavic Manuscripts handed down to us, which reach back as far as the X. century, are rather numerous, thanks to the almost complete state of preservation of the libraries and treasuries of the many old cloisters in Russia. Besides there is an important collection of manuscripts at the Imperial Public Library of St. Petersburgh and at the library of the Synodal printing works of Moscow.

On table 31 we have added to the patterns of Byzantine Ornaments some examples of manuscript-painting found in Russian libraries, dating from the X., up to the XIII. century. In connection therewith our table 33a represents a considerable number of characteristic examples from the XIV. and

Fig. 18.

XV., centuries, during which the style of Russian manuscript-painting was most flourishing. This period is marked by the assertion on the one side of braided work displayed on a geometrical base and on the other side of more unconstrained motives combined with animal forms which remind us of Celtic ornaments. The few pigments used of these occasions are as a rule confined to blue, red, yellow and green. This simplicity of colour, together with a symmetrical order of forms, confers a most agreeable calm on the manuscript-paintings in question; the motives of that time are still employed for coloured letter-press, Enamels and similar technics.

Figure 1. From a Gospel of the XIV. Century in the Imperial Public Library.
    „   2, 3, 12 and 13. From Psalteries in the library of the Trinity Cloister near Moscow.
    „   4 and 5. From Psalteries in the Imperial Public Library.
    „   6 and 7. From Gospels in the Rumjantzoff Museum, Moscow.
    „   8. Book-ornament, XV. Century from Rostow.
    „   9 and 15. From a prayer book in the Cloister of Miracles, Moscow.
    „   10 and 11. Fractions of alphabetical characters. XIV. Century.
    „   14. From a prayer book in the Bjeloserski Cloister XV. Century.
    „   16. From a Gospel in the Cloister of Marys glorification near Nowgorod.
    „   17. From a Psaltery of the XV. Century.
    „   18. Book-ornament from the work »Appendice à l'imitation de Jésus-Christ.«
    „   19. From a Gospel XII. Century in the Rumjantzoff Museum, Moscow.

The table is arranged by M. Scherwinsky, Director of the Industrial school, Riga.
Taken from „The publication of the Moscow Museum of Art Industry" and from „W. Stassow, Slavic Ornament in old and new manuscripts".
„History of Russian Ornaments from the X. to the XIV. Century. Museum of Art Industry at Moscow" and „Appendice à l'imitation de Jésus-Christ".

Fig. 19.

Table 34 B.

RUSSIA.

ARCHITECTURAL ORNAMENTS AND WOOD-CARVINGS.

As regards their form and decoration the oldest Russian buildings resemble closely the Byzantine monuments which is explained by the fact, that it was from Byzantium that the Gospel was carried to and extended over Russia in the IX. Century. These Russian-Byzantine structures certainly do not lack original motives which were improved upon in Russia, but in many cases it is almost impossible to trace them to their source. Many forms of this style, and especially of the distinct Russian style of the XVI. Century may no doubt be regarded as importations from the far East. The Russian style flourished until the XVIII. Century only, when french influences began to assert themselves there as all over Europe.

Fig. 22.

One of the most prominent and peculiar buildings of the XVI. Century is the church of Saint Basil at Moscow (built in memory of the capture of Kasan). The forms of the XVI. Century are frequently adopted for modern constructions in the Russian style.

Characteristical in Russian churches are their bulbiform cupolas (Fig. 1) which we see in a variety of shapes. The baldaquins in most places of worship present a particularly rich configuration; we often find them crowned with keel-like gables and turrets, reminding us somewhat of Gothic superstructures. (Fig. 4.) Not seldom we come across arched ornaments meeting between the chief supports which rest upon a bordered favorite towels which in Russia garnish the portraits of Saints or looking glasses etc. For this reason the said ornamental boards are populary called „towels". —

richly embellished tenon. (Fig. 3.) Very abundant are motives for wood-architecture on the farmhouses in the central and northern governments. Their origin often is a very ancient one. It is astonishing to notice the severe style of these ornaments which consist of planed boards artfully perforated and sawn out, and to consider the uniform punctuality bestowed on the work. A favorite hobby are the ornamental boards suspended from the projecting cornices of the roofs (Fig. 11, 12 and 13) and also employed as an embellishment underneath the outside sills of the windows. Frequently they are brightened up with colours and thus look at a distance like those richly embroidered and lace-

We willingly recognize, that Russian architecture deserves our special appreciation and are glad to observe that its native Country has since a few years by means of meritorious publications, directed the attention of the Public at large to this highly interesting style of architecture.

Fig. 1. Phantastic church-cupolas at Jaroslaw. XVII. and XVIII. Century.
„ 2 and 3. Gilt wood carvings of the Baldaquin of the Imperial chair in the Nicolay church. Jaroslaw. XVII. Century.
„ 4. From a baldaquin in the Museum of the Imperial Academy of Arts.
„ 5 and 6. Carved roses on the principal door of the altar, church of St. John, near Rostow, XVII. Century.
„ 7—10. Window frames of wooden houses in the government Wologda.
„ 11—13. Gable ornaments in the same district.
„ 14 and 15. Ornamental Boards on sills etc.
„ 16—19. Roses on the wings of doors, made of small panels. Government of Samara.
„ 20 and 21. Portions of such roses.
„ 22. Capital with vegetable ornaments.

The figures 1, 4 and 15—21 after copies taken by M. Scherwinsky, Director of the Industrial School at Riga. The remaining figures are taken from:
„Prince Gagarin, Collection of Byzantine and Old-russian Ornaments."
„l'Architecte, St. Petersbourg, 1885," and
„Viollet-le-Duc, L'art russe."

Printed by A. Gatternicht, Stuttgart, Germany.

MANUSCRIPT-PAINTING.

ARCHITECTURAL ORNAMENTS AND WOOD-CARVINGS.

Table 34^C.

RUSSIA.

ENAMEL, MAJOLIKA, PAINTINGS ON WALLS AND CEILINGS, JAPANNED WOODWORK.

In Russia we find *enamel ornaments* on gold, silver and copper still as widely distributed and as highly esteemed as in former times when they first attained their reputation. The figures 15—18 present some interesting examples of this kind and it is especially figure 15 which shows us how extensive was the employment of these noble technics, for here we see the edge of a gold dish belonging to a set for 120 persons which Czar Alexei Michaelowitsch (1645—1676) is said to have had manufactured by Russian artists.

In like manner have the Majolica technics found an early and extensive employment in consequence of their being preferred and used for the ornamentation of the fronts of Palaces and churches no less than of the interior of altars, but most particularly of stoves in private rooms. This we find confirmed in many towns along the river Volga, especially at Jaroslaw, by an abundance of examples. In recent times these beautiful technics have been taken up again in many parts of Russia and the result has been a highly satisfactory one.

Fig. 22.

As to ornamental painting on *walls* and *ceilings,* the old remnants which Russia can furnish are not very numerous. They present to us tender creepers with large leaves and flowers in deep colours which betray an Oriental origin, and some of them are enlivened by portrait-medaillons interspersed.

One of the most interesting branches of the house-industries still to this day practised in the central parts of Russia, is the production of *japanned wood articles* which possess great durability. (Fig. 19—21.) These utensils first receive a surface of precipitate of graphite upon which the patterns are painted-generally in black or red colours and finally they are coated with linseed oil boiled down to a jelly. This latter confers a greenish gold tint on the graphite which imparts a rich and warm colouring to the articles thus treated.

Fig. 1—4. Wall-paintings on a spiral staircase in the Cathedral of the Annunciation at Moscow. XV. Century.

„ 5—7. Ornaments on vaults in a house of Moscow. XVII. Century.

„ 8 and 9. Majolica-Pilaster as window frame at the Terem (Palace of the Empresses) on the Kreml, Moscow.

„ 10—14. Stove-pans made in the market-town of Ustjug. XVII. Century, in the Museum of the Imperial Society for the promotion of Art in St. Petersburgh.

„ 15. Edge of a gold dish in the treasury of the Kreml at Moscow.

„ 16—18. Veil from the portrait of a saint of the XVII. Century. Enamel on silver. From the Museum of the Imperial Society for the promotion of Art, St. Petersburgh.

„ 19—21. Japanned wooden spoons and top of a footstool. Articles made by peasants in the district of Nowgorod.

„ 22. Ornament in chased metal.

Fig. 19—21 after copies made by M. Scherwinsky. Director of the Industrial School at Riga.
The other subjects taken from:
„N. Simakof: l'ornement russe dans les anciens produits de l'art industriel national.“
„Th. Sonzew: „Altertümer des russischen Kaiserreiches, Moskau 1849—1853.“
„Viollet-le-Duc: l'art russe.“

Fig. 25.

Table 34 D.

NORTHERN.

WOOD-CARVING.

If we devote a chapter to the »Northern style« it is by no means our intention to embody in our table every variation of style appertaining to this category, which succeeded each other from the roman-germanic period down to the introduction of Christianity. Our representations, on the contrary, are confined to the time this side of the twelfth century.

We have already on Table 30, when speaking of *Celtic ornaments*, expressed our opinion that the same betray original and independent characteristics and that traces of this style may be noticed more especially in Scandinavia. In the same manner as Irish missionaries, animated by an enthusiastic migratory impulse, disseminated the Irish style over the whole of Western Europe, its introduction in Northern countries and particularly in Norway took place as far back as the VIII. century. It was then that motives of the oldest Irish style began to be most intimately blended with the style introduced by the migration of nations (Charlemagne) which had up to that time been dominant in the North. Thus a peculiar compound style was created and this developed — especially in the IX. Century during the Viking period with its Northern ascendancy — to that so-called *northern-irish* style which testifies to Icelands artistic influence up to the XI. Century. In the same manner as animal ornaments used to form the universal basis of style in comtemporaneous west- and northeuropean Art, so do above all animal motives play an important part also in scandinavian Art. At first they represented an intricate surface decoration loaded with animal figures, difficult to unravel but free from any admixture of other motives. Later on foreign elements are added in the form of quadruped animals, birds, snakes, images of lions and winged dragons, which are changed into novel and strange forms of animals conformably with the earliest mediaeval style. These varied animal motives are then encompassed by all sorts of foliage and tape-like motives. The foliaceous ornaments, elaborated in romanish fashion, were gradually enlarged to such extent that the original style was thereby forced into other paths more in sympathy with the traditions of Greek Art. No symbolic attributes whatever attach to the animal figures here introduced, for they must simply be taken as ornamental motives. At free terminal points, such as gableheads, waterspouts, ships'-prows etc. as also at the upper termination of pilastres human ad animal heads or birds were preferably made use of. (Fig. 13—16.) Frequently we also meet with original ornaments composed of letters and with that score- or notch-work so widely adopted for minor objects of Art.

Fig. 24.

We possess moreover a rich store of northern ornaments in those wooden churchs of the XII. and XIII. Centuries which are still to be found in Sweden and Norway. Whilst we learn from those how ornamental Art was applied to buildings, we at the same time are impressed by the infinite exactness which characterized the Art of wood-carving in those times as practised on the most varied domestic articles, many of those being even enchased in colours. as may be seen in the Museums of Art industry at Copenhagen, Stockholm, Christiania etc.

As regards the technics in relation thereto, we have to consider the fact that these ornaments were one and all carved with knives which was of no little influence on the formation of the plain relievo-ornaments here adopted.

Figure 1. Porch of the church at Hedal.	Figure 12. Portion of a stall in the choir of same church.
„ 2. Side portion of the Porch of the church at Austad.	„ 13. Upper termination of a pilaster in the church of Gol.
„ 3. The same of the church at Hyllestad.	„ 14. Swedish ships-prow in the Museum of Christiania.
„ 4. Arches of the Arcades in the church at Opdal (Numedal).	„ 15 and 16. Waterspout on the church at Moere.
„ 5 and 6. Scrolls of cylindrical capitals of pillars in the church at Lomen.	„ 18—23. Swedish notch-ornaments in the Nordland Museum at Stockholm.
„ 7. Gallery in the church at Hurum.	„ 24. Side portion of the porch of the church at Urnes.
„ 8 and 9. Scrolls of cylindrical capitals of pillars in the same church.	„ 25. Frieze in the church at Opdal.
„ 10 and 11. Capitals in the church at Urnes.	

Taken from: „Ruprich-Robert, l'architecture normande." „Tidskrift for Kunstindustri." „Oldenburg, träsniderimönster ur Nordiska Museet i Stockholm." „Dietrichson, de norske stavkirker." „Mindesmerker af Middelalderens Kunst i Norge "

ENAMEL, MAJOLIKA, PAINTINGS ON WALLS AND CEILINGS,
JAPANNED WOODWORK.

WOOD-CARVING.

Plate 35.

MIDDLE-AGES.

ENAMEL AND ILLUMINATION OF MANUSCRIPTS.

The Romanesque ornament found its freeest display in the illumination of manuscripts, where particularly the large initials were magnificently treated (Fig. 1 and 2). Especially animals were here combined with scroll work in the most strange arabesque-like representations. The ground of the paintings in earlier times was gold, later on many-coloured.

In the art of enamelling, which had been transferred from Byzantium to Germany, the German artists attained a high point of perfection; only they took for their metal-ground copper-plates instead of the expensive gold-plates, and instead of "émail cloisonné" they employed "champlevé work" which then spread also in France and made especially the manufacturies of Limoges far and wide renowned. — Generally, when figural representations were designed, the artists treated only the background and the surrounding ornaments in this manner, sparing out the figures themselves in metal and after having engraved the details (contours of garments etc.) with the burin, raised their effect by coloured enamel. (Compare the head in Fig. 20.) Fig. 3 shows a somewhat different kind of enamelling, the contours themselves being spared out, and the remainder of the figure worked in enamel. The prominent head is made of gilt copper, as in many such objects of art, and put on separately. Fig. 6 and 11 show the zigzag and circular — arched mouldings, so much favoured in architecture.

Fig. 1. Initial from a German manuscript (Rhenish school), XI. — XII. cent., in the Library at Paris.
„ 2. Initial from a German manuscript of the XII. cent. from a private collection at Cologne.
„ 3. Relic-cross from the first half of the XII. cent. in the Diöcesan-Museum at Freising.
„ 4. Pilaster from the shrine of St. Heribertus in the Benedictine-Abbey at Deutz. Midst of the XII. cent.
„ 5 and 10. From the shrive of the great relics at Aachen. XII. cent.
„ 6. From a collection at Bonn. XII. cent.
„ 7. Decoration from the Anno-shrine in the former abbey at Siegburg. XI. cent.
„ 8 and 9. From a reliquary in South-Kensington Museum at London. XII. cent.
„ 11. From a little reliquary. XII. cent.
„ 12 and 13. From the portable altar of St. Andrews in the cathedral at Treves. X. cent.
„ 14. Flat disk of gilt copper in private possession at Bamberg. XII. cent.
„ 15. Half from a shrine in the former abbey at Siegburg. XI. cent.
„ 16—19. Decorations on double crosses at Essen. XI. cent.
„ 20. Half figure of an angel from the shrine of St. Heribertus. Vide Fig. 4.
„ 21. From the shrine of Charlemagne at Aachen. XII. cent.
„ 22 and 23. From the Mauritius-shrine at Siegburg. XI. cent.
„ 24. From an altar-wall. XII. cent.

Plate 36.

MIDDLE-AGES.

WALL PAINTING.

The colours used in wall painting are cheerful and of great variety. The human figures do not exhibit the same rigidity of old age as the contemporary Byzantine, but show a freeer and more youthful movement. The folds of the garments following pretty closely the forms of the body, are much better modelled than, for instance, in the Byzantine images. As regards the ornament, all the pecularities of the Romanesque style we have mentioned hitherto, are likewise applicable to it. Frequent use is made of the circle or parts of a circle.

Fig. 1 and 2. From the apsis of the Basilica di S. Angelo in Formis near Capua. XI. century.

„ 3—5. From the chapter-house of the former Benedictine-abbey Brauweiler near Cologne. XI. century.

„ 6—9. From the lower church at Schwarz-Rheindorf near Bonn. Midst of the XII. century.

„ 10, 11 and 15. From the choir of the cathedral at Braunschweig. XII. century.

„ 12. From the former abbey-church at Marcigny. XII. century.

„ 13 and 14. From the church at Anzy. XII. century.

„ 16 and 17. From the lower church S. Francesco at Assisi.

Printed by Max Seeger, Stuttgart, Germany.

ENAMEL AND ILLUMINATION OF MANUSGRIPTS.

Printed by K. Hochdanz, Stuttgart, Germany.

WALL PAINTING.

Plate 37.

MIDDLE-AGES.

STAINED GLASS.

Although the production of coloured glass was already known in the 9th century, we cannot speak of glass-painting before the close of the 10th century. At that time the first trials were made to shade glass

panes, stained in the substance, by melting a darker colour upon them, and in the 13th century the makers proceeded to cover or "flash" colourless glass (which had, however, always a greenish-yellow hue), with coloured glass and to engrave the design on to the latter, so that according to the requirements the flashed glass had more or less thickness in some places or was even entirely removed. Then these colourless places were often still

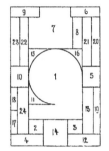

painted with another colour, and in order to produce a greater richness of coloration different colours were laid on both sides of the glass. — Finally the finished glasses were joined by lead-rods so as to form the required design.

In the Romanesque period glass-paintings still bear quite the character of carpets, the place of which they in reality supply. The window-surface is covered with ribbon and leaf

ornaments, in the midst of which, we find however, very early medallions with little figural representations; less frequently we meet with standing figures, filling up the whole window. The single figures are still clumsy and wrongly drawn.

Fig. 1—6. From the cathedral at Chartres.
,, 7. ,, ,, abbey-church at St. Denis.
.. 8. ,, ,, church St. Urbain at Troyes.
,, 9. ,, ,, cathedral ibid.
,, 10. ,, ,, ,, at Laon.
,, 11 and 12. From the cathedral at Angers.
.. 13 and 14. ,, ,, Samaritan church at Bourges.
,, 15. ,, ,, cathedral ibid.
,, 16. ,, ,, ,, at Châlons.
,, 17 and 18. ,, ,, St. Chapelle at Paris.
,, 19. ,, ,, minster of Strassburg.
,. 20—23. ,, ,, choir of the upper church S. Francesco at Assisi.
,, 24. ,. ,, church S. Paolo fuori le mura at Rome (modern).

Plate 38.

MIDDLE-AGES.

STONE-MOSAIC.

Where stones of various colours for an artistic floor-incrustation were not available, it plainly was expedient, to use small clay-plates or engraved stone-flags for adorning the floors. Such stone-flags, with the designs executed in coloured cement, we met with already, when speaking of the Arabian ornamentation, likewise with small clay-tiles joined together as a kind of mosaic-flooring (Fig. 9—16). In the latter case we find, especially in the period of the predominance of Romanesque style, either each single colour represented by a corresponding little plate (Fig. 13—16), or the ornament impressed on a clay-plate, the ridges filled up with variously coloured cement, and the whole finally faced with transparent glazing, (Fig. 17—27).

Besides this, there came up the custom, which spread especially in the Gothic period, of drawing on the separate tiles a sunk or raised design by means of a model. It took usually four of these little plates put together to form the intended ornament; they were left in their natural colour and frequently glazed.

In the mosaic-like composition we meet, of course, almost exclusively with simple geometrical patterns, whereas, in the other kinds of floor-incrustation mentioned above, human figures, animals and plants are chiefly represented. Among the plants the lily is most variously idealised, and as in glass-painting, the oak and wine leaves which are everywhere repeated.

Fig. 1—8. Engraved stone-flags from the old cathedral at St. Omer, XIII. century (ground brown, interior design of horse and horseman filled up with red).

" 9 and 10. Mosaic floors of burnt clay, enamelled, from a collection at Dresden (black and red centres with white edging) XIII. century.

" 11 and 12. Mosaic floors of burnt clay, enamelled, from the cloister-church Colombe-les-Sens (red, black and yellow), XII. century.

" 13 and 14. Mosaic floors of burnt clay, enamelled, from the abbey-church at St. Denis (red, black and yellow), XII. century.

" 15 and 16. Mosaic floors of burnt clay, enamelled, from the old abbey-church at Pontigny, XII. century (yellow, red and black on green ground).

" 17—23. Enamelled clay-tiles from St. Pierre-sur-Dive, XII. century (yellow and black-brown).

" 24 and 25. " " " from the church at Bloxham, XIII. century (red and yellow).

" 26 and 27. " " " from Beddington-Church in Surrey, XV. century (red and yellow).

" 28. Engraved clay-tiles from the town-hall at Ravensburg (natural colour without glazing), XIV. century.

" 29. Engraved clay-tiles from a patrician house ibid., XIV. century.

" 30. Clay-tiles with deepened ground, natural colour without glazing, XIV. century, from the church at Gaildorf.

" 31. Clay-tiles with deepened ground and relief-figures from the cloister at Alpirsbach, XII. cent.

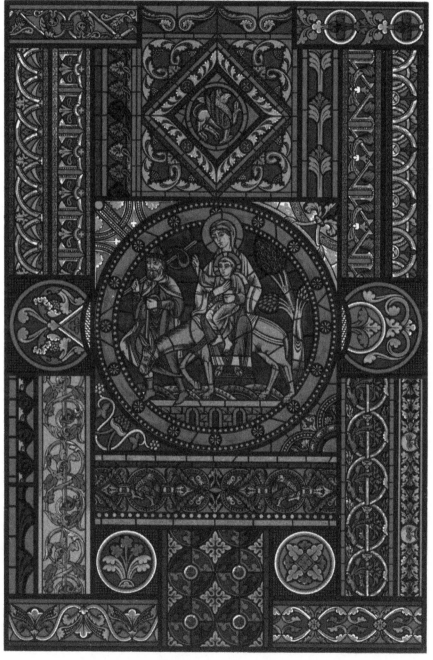

Printed by K. Hochdanz, Stuttgart, Germany.

STAINED GLASS.

Printed by E. Hochdanz, Stuttgart, Germany.

STONE MOSAIC.

Plate 39.

MIDDLE-AGES.

WOOD MOSAIC.

I̤t was no great step from adorning walls and floors with variously coloured materials to a similar decoration of wooden objects. Here however, ornamentation was somewhat limited by the nature of wood; accordingly vegetable and figural representations are seldom found, at least in the Gothic style, whereas we meet most frequently with band and line ornament, in conjunction with a kind of mosaic work, consisting of small pieces of wood being arranged as stars, etc.

Fig. 1—6. From a reading-desk in the cathedral of Orvieto.
  „ 7 and 8. From the stalls of Frari Church at Venice.
  „ 9—17. From the vestry-door in S. Anastasia at Verona.
  „ 18—27. From the stalls in the minster at Ulm.

Plate 40.

MIDDLE-AGES.

STAINED GLASS.

Whereas in the Romanesque period purely ornamental decorations were chiefly executed, these however in most perfect style, there took place a great change in this regard, during the 14th century. When the Romanesque style of glass-painting, after having prevailed far into the Gothic period, was now completely superseded, the artists were induced to fill up the wide window-openings principally with figural ornament. The carpet-patterns, so much in favour formerly, were more and more employed only as a back-ground for the figures, a lofty architecture being added. The idealised foliage and scroll work however, still takes its place as a border; but being treated more and more freely later on, it frequently degenerates into wild extravagance. However, besides the windows with figural representations, we also find some purely ornamented a special kind of which, termed "grisailles", is decorated with a black design on colourless glass, other colours usually being used but sparingly.

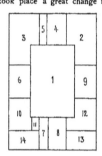

Fig. 1. From a choir-window in the minster of Ulm.

„ 2 and 3. From the choir-windows of the Frauenkirche at Esslingen.

„ 4—8. In the National Museum at Munich, formerly in the cathedral of Regensburg.

„ 9. From a choir-window in the cathedral of Cologne.

„ 10 and 11. From the choir of the cloister-church at Königsfelden (Switzerland).

„ 12. From one of the aisle-windows of the upper church S. Francesco at Assisi.

„ 13 and 14. From the side-aisle-windows of the lower church ibid.

Printed by Max Seeger, Stuttgart, Germany.

WOOD MOSAIC.

Printed by K. Hochdanz, Stuttgart, Germany.

STAINED GLASS.

Plate 41.

MIDDLE-AGES.

ORNAMENTAL ARCHITECTURE AND SCULPTURE.

In the Gothic style we find throughout (setting aside the degenerations of the latest Gothic period) the decorations subordinate to the architecture. Therefore, according to this principle, the ornament nowhere predominates over the architectonic structure, it never becomes independent, but serves only to supplement harmoniously the impression of the architecture, or to mark out single mouldings according to requirement. In this way especially the pointed-arched portal-gates and windows, the boldly-rising towers and turrets, the pinnacles etc. etc., the capitals and cornices, the stalls and galleries have ornamental decoration, with which also the works of the small art, such as household-furniture and sacred utensils are not at all sparingly supplied.

The capitals of the columns represent in most cases only a bell-shaped enlargement of the shaft, around which leaves and flowers are wound in a free style (Fig. 15—17). In general the employment of vegetable decoration is very extended; for instance the crockets on the edges of the gables and tower-pyramids are in reality nothing else than leaves freely transformed; likewise the key-stones of the vaults, the consols etc. are very frequently adorned with foliage.

From the manner of treatment of these leaves and flowers can be determined pretty nearly to which period a building or a piece of furniture belongs. For, whereas in the first Gothic period (XIII. century) a full and large treatment prevails, idealising the natural forms, only slightly (Fig. 4, 5, 6, 15, 16, 21), later on a bolder execution gains ground (Fig. 10—12); whilst in the last Gothic period a gradual departure from the natural forms is evident, all foliage having a knotty appearane, which produces on the one side a certain rigidness (Fig. 8, 9, 22), on the other sometimes a want of repose (Fig. 17, 18, 20). This want arises particularly also from the common practice of undercutting the leaves so freely, that they appear scarcely affixed, the consequence of which is frequently a too hard change of light and shade.

The foliage of the native plants is in special favour. Everywhere we meet with the leaves of the vine, thistle, oak and beech, of ivy and trefoil, of roses etc., most of these plants being symbolically used.

Human figures and animals are often humorously employed in the so-called water-spouts; also consols, key-stones and particularly the pediments above the doors are adorned with figural representations.

Fig. 1. Carved figure from the stalls of the Minster at Ulm.
  „ 2. Projecting bracket of a seat-flap (Misericordia) of the same stalls.
  „ 3. Key-stone-decoration from the cathedral at Naumburg.
  „ 4. Projecting bracket of a capital from the church at Gelnhausen.
  „ 5. „   „ „ „ of French origin.
  „ 6. Finial from Notre-dame at Paris.
  „ 7. Knob of a finial ibid.
  „ 8. Finial from the tabernacle of the former hospital-church at Esslingen.
  „ 9. Crocket from Nuremberg.
  „ 10. „   „ Cologne Cathedral.
  „ 11 and 12. Hollow-decoration ibid.
  „ 13 and 14. Water-spout ibid.
  „ 15. Capital of French origin.
  „ 16. „ from the cloister of the church at Wimpfen-im-Thal.
  „ 17. „ from the bell-hall of the ‚Frauenkirche‘ at Esslingen.
  „ 18. „ from the font in the ‚Marienkirche‘ at Reutlingen.
  „ 19. Cornice-decoration on the cathedral of Troyes.
  „ 20. Carved and pierced panel of a little shrine-door of French origin.
  „ 21. Hollow-decoration from the church at Wimpfen-im-Thal.
  „ 22. „   „ from Nuremberg.

Plate 42.

MIDDLE-AGES.

WEAVING, EMBROIDERY, ENAMEL AND POLYCHROME SCULPTURE.

Weavings and embroideries, a great number of which were, during the Gothic period, made especially in monasteries, followed at first the examples from the South and East (Fig. 11). But this imitation was more and more rejected, and preference given to decoration with flowers and leaves, rigorously idealised without excluding the figural element. The latter was employed specially in ecclesiastical robes, curtains and carpets in churches, where they involved a symbolical meaning.

If we bear in mind the influence exercised in earlier times by the Byzantine and Arabian art, we cannot wonder, that the linear ornament preserved its place in the Italian Gothic style (Fig. 6—9. Compare also Plate 44, fig. 13, 14, 16, 19).

Wood or stone sculptures were frequently painted, in which case the patterns of the robes usually show the above mentioned motives.

Fig. 12 and 13 pertain already to the transition of the Gothic to the Renaissance style.

Enamel was most richly applied to the splendid reliquaries, especially in the 13th century; here, however, the Romanesque forms of decoration still prevailed.

Fig. 1. Statue of St. Simon in the choir of Cologne Cathedral.
 „ 2. Pattern on the robe of another statue ibid.
 „ 3. Embroidered fonder of French origin. XIV. century.
 „ 4. Embroidered stuff (in the original, silver is employed instead of gold). XV. cent.
 „ 5. „ „ XIV. cent.
 „ 6—9. Borders and patterns of carpets from the wall-paintings in the upper church S. Francesco at Assisi. XIV. cent.
 „ 10. Pattern of a carpet from a tempera-painting of Niccolo Alunno (1466) in the pinacotheca at Perugia.
 „ 11. Sicilian weaving from St. Mary's church at Danzig. XIII. cent.
 „ 12. Border of a carpet on the painting of Hugo van der Goes in the Palazzo degli Uffizi at Florence. XV. cent.
 „ 13. „ „ „ „ on a picture of Mantegna in S. Zeno at Verona. Close of the XV. cent.
 „ 14. Border from an embroidered chasuble. XIV. cent. (German work).
 „ 15 and 16. Patterns of stuffs from the XIV. cent., of French origin.
 „ 17. Gilt copper-engraving from the cross-relics-table in the catholic parish-church at Mettlach.
 „ 18—20. Enamelled decorations on the shrine of the Three Kings in Cologne Cathedral. Beginning of the XIII. cent.
 „ 21. Enamelled border from the beginning of the XIII. cent. in the Musée de Cluny.

Printed by Max Seeger, Stuttgart, Germany.

ORNAMENTAL ARCHITECTURE AND SCULPTURE.

—

Printed by K. Hochdanz, Stuttgart, Germany.

WEAVING, EMBROIDERY, ENAMEL AND POLYCHROME SCULPTURE.

Plate 43.

MIDDLE-AGES.

ILLUMINATION OF MANUSCRIPTS.

I n the illumination of manuscripts the livelier forms of the ornament superseded slowly the round, surface-filling forms of the Romanesque style. The flowers were partly idealised, also some direct from nature, and Figs. 8 and 13 give us an idea how both kinds of treatment were often combined, especially in the later Gothic time. Characteristically of this time is a deep shading, as well as the use of half tones, and the laying on of lights.

Remarkable is the variety and splendour of the colours which represent the abundance and brightness of the flowers in the miniatures of the venerable manuscripts of that age.

Fig. 1—4. From the XIV. century.

„ 5—13. With the single leaves and flowers from the XV. century.

Plate 44.

MIDDLE-AGES.

CEILING AND WALL PAINTING.

The further progress in wall-painting in the Gothic period was somewhat impeded by the want of wall-surfaces suitable to the reception of larger pictures, whereas sufficient opportunity was given for ornamentation. — The occurring figures were influenced by the upward direction and the frequent narrowness of the space at disposal, wherefore they exhibit not seldom a too slender appearance. But differing from the Romanesque figures, nearly all of them show a certain life and grace in attitude and gesture, which led, however, in the further development to somewhat tortuous and mannered postures. (Compare Fig. 4 and Plate 42, Fig. 1.) — The folds of the robes flow softly down in long, beautiful lines, the outlines of the drapery are black and there occurs very little shading with variegated colours. In Fig. 1 shading is done with black hatching. Fig. 17 gives an example of the way in which the Antique begins to ascend and to lead into the Renaissance.

Fig. 22.

Fig. 1. From a pedigree in the hospital-church at Stuttgart. XV. century.
   „ 2. Portion of Fig. 22. Painted flat ornament, the ground being deepened.
   „ 3 and 4. From the church at Brauweiler. XIV. cent.
   „ 5. From a chapel at Ramersdorf. XIV. cent.
   „ 6 and 7. From a side-room in the collegiate church at Fritzlar. XV. cent.
   „ 8. From the Jacobine-church at Agen. XIII. cent.
   „ 9 and 10. From the Ste. Chapelle at Paris. XIII. cent.
   „ 11—19.   „   „ upper church San Francesco at Assisi.
   „ 20 and 21.   „   „ lower church ibid.
   „ 22. (Vide the above text-illustration.) Lower wied of the wood-baldachin above the former abbot-seat in the convent-church at Blaubeuren.

ILLUMINATION OF MANUSCRIPTS.

CEILING- AND WALL-PAINTING.

Plate 45.

ITALIAN RENAISSANCE.

GLASS PAINTING.

In the Gothic period already, the practise of filling in the window-openings (apertures) entirely with coloured glasses, declined more and more. In the place of these came, (especially in the beginning of the Rennaissance style,) small glass paintings on colourless ground, which were however encircled with borders and framings, often so elaborately ornamented that these seem to form the chief decoration, the subjects of which are generally plants and animals, but often also of human figures. Neither are all kinds of symbolic subjects and figures wanting, as a glance at the annexed plate shows; but these certainly belong to a later time of the Rennaissance period.

Fig. 1. From the National Museum in the Bargello at Florence, taken by H. Dolmetsch.

„ 2—8. From the Certosa near Florence (by Giovanni da Udine), taken by Reg.-Baumeister Borkhardt and Architect Eckert in Stuttgart.

Plate 46.

ITALIAN RENAISSANCE.

POLYCHROME POTTERY.

It was a natural consequence of the material of glazed clay-plates and of the way of making them, that floors and wainscots consisting of such little plates could not present an ornament so minutely and elaborately finished as works of metal, marble etc. Therefore, when this "technique" goes beyond the simple geometric pattern, the ornaments, which for the most part bear resemblance to Byzantine and Oriental models are rather modest, but all the more clear and vigorous. Their effect, however, is still increased by the excellent combination of colours, although, in wise moderation, rarely more than 4 colours were used.

In the manufacture of such tile-floors and wainscot-plates, the school of Della Robbia attained special celebrity, wherefore such plate-mosaics are frequently registered under the name of "Robbian ware".

Fig. 1, 6, 9, 11, 12, 13, 14 and 15. Wainscot-plates on the staircaise-walls of the house Nr. 26 in Via Luccoli at Genoa.

„ 2, 3, 4, 5, 7, 8 and 10. The same in the house Nr. 10 in Via S. Matteo ibid.

„ 16 and 17. Floor-plates from San Petronio at Bologna.

45

Printed by K. Hochdanz. Stuttgart. Germany.

Plate 47.

ITALIAN RENAISSANCE.

ORNAMENTAL PAINTING.

It was at the commencement of the 15th century, that the Renaissance style began to make its appearance in Italy, and the period till about 1500 may be called the period of Early Renaissance, in contradistinction of High Renaissance which lasted till the middle of the 16th century.

Renaissance is a new adaptation, not a servile imitation, but a free treatment of antique forms; the plainest evidence of this is given by the ornament, of which this style makes a richer and ampler use than any other. This applies more particularly to the motives we meet with; and here we observe above all the vegetable ornament, which in Early Renaissance generally covers the ground only moderately. We find almost everywhere delicate, beautifully curved branches in a symmetrical or at least regular arrangement, in which the antique acanthus-leaf acts the principal part, although, not without the most various transformations. Also vine, laurel, ivy etc. are frequently employed, partly copying nature directly, partly idealised. But this foliage with its branches and fruit is still enlivened by a rich variation of animals, fantastical beings, human figures as well as symbolical subjects, arms, masks, emblems, vases, candelabras etc. Most cultivated is the combination of human figures and animals with vegetable elements (Fig. 3; compare also plate 45). Finally a not less important part of the decoration are coats of arms and escutcheons, the latter usually as so-called horse-front-shields (Fig. 6 and 9) in the period of Early Renaissance, later on as cartouches.

All we mentioned hitherto is found in facade-painting, i. e. in those paintings with which the fronts of single houses, for want of plastic adornment, were entirely faced, showing either ornaments or historical representations. The colours are bright and harmoniously composed, so that a gorgeous impression results from such architecture often not only coloured but really painted. From a later period, when the many-figured historical representations almost wholly superseded the ornament, one often finds fronts painted in bronze-colour or in grisaille.

Fig. 1–7. From the front of a house in Genoa (Via San Matteo. Nr, 10).
  „ 8.   Front of the court of „Casa Taverna' at Milan.
  „ 9–11. „ „ „ r „ Palazzo Piccolomini at Pienza.

Plate 48.

ITALIAN RENAISSANCE.

WOOD MOSAIC.

Wood-carving in general was highly flourishing, as is known, in the Renaissance-period, especially however (in the highest degree) one branch of it, termed Intarsia, i. e. inlaid wood-work, with which stalls, shrines in vestries etc., were most richly decorated. As far as the represented subjects are concerned there is actually no restriction, for we meet with a great variety of complete pictures as well as perspective views and ornaments. The latter, for the most part light on dark ground, present us a splendid abundance of idealised vegetable motives, mixed or combined with various vases, vessels, living beings etc. The arrangement of the scroll-work is strictly symmetrical, at least on regular, framed surfaces, where also the acanthus-leaf is in the first place made use of, but it is singular to observe, that the points of the leaves are influenced by the mode of making them.

In order to work out more life, sometimes Niello is employed next the Intarsia; the ribs of the leaves, the hatching etc. are produced by the application of a dark composition.

Fig. 1.   From the choir-stalls in S. Anastasia at Verona.

„ 2.   From the dado of the vestry-shrines in S. Maria in Organo ibid.

„ 3—7.   From the choir-stalls ibid.

„ 8.   From the choir-stalls in Monte Oliveto maggiore.

„ 9 u. 10. „   „   „   „   in S. Petronio at Bologna. (Ground of the centre-compartments black).

„ 11—13. „   „   „   „   in the Certosa near Pavia. (In Fig. 12 ground black).

Printed by Max Berger Stuttgart, Germany.

ORNAMENTAL PAINTING.

Printed by E. Hochdanz, Stuttgart, Germany.

WOOD-MOSAIC.

Plate 49.

ITALIAN RENAISSANCE.

CEILING PAINTING.

With the ceilings of churches and palaces, whether arched or horizontal wood-ceilings, a rich field of activity was opened to the genius of artists. The most distinguished masters did not disdain to improve the ornamentation by framing their frescoes with decorations of their own invention (Fig. 1 and 2). In these ornaments, vegetable and animal motives being mixed, the ground is mostly light, the colours themselves being cheerful and bright. — Besides these, however, more simple patterns are not wanting. Where figural representations are missing, their place is supplied by painted cassettes or rosettes, edged with geometrical ornaments. — It is noticeable how such coloured ornaments are combined with more or less simple stucco decorations, the latter however being often, as in Fig. 1, strikingly imitated with the brush. The two rosettes (Fig. 11 and 12) certainly belong, in respect of their origin, to a period antecedent to that of Renaissance, but in their formation they already show an evident affinity with Renaissance itself.

Fig. 1—4. From the choir-arch in S. Maria del Popolo at Rome. (By Pinturicchio.)

„ 5. From one of the Borgia chambers in the Vatican at Rome.

„ 6 and 9. Patterns from the arch-panels in the Certosa near Pavia.

„ 7 and 10. Borders round these panels.

„ 11 and 12 medaillons from the arch-panels in S. Francesco at Lodi.

Plate 50.

ITALIAN RENAISSANCE.

LACES.

The art of lace-making, unknown to the ancients, and no doubt, not brought to artistic perfection previously to the close of the 15th century, may truly be called a creation of the Renaissance. And it is the soil of Italy, principally the two cities of Venice and Genoa, to which we owe the needle-made lace as well as the finest kind of pillow-lace. The former (the so-called point) is to be considered as the more precious kind. The method of making it — ground and ornament consisting of nothing but an infinity of stitches made à jour — admits of an extremely delicate and graceful formation. But its execution requires a very complicated and difficult process, as only small pieces of about 10 cm dimension can be made at a time, which, after being done, must be joined so as to form a complete whole, for which reason, in designing the patterns, the possibility of a scarcely visible joining of the several parts must be taken into account. The most esteemed of the sewed laces is the Venetian point in relief, all leaves, flowers etc. which show raised edges. A still higher degree of perfection in this kind of lace is attained in work with leaves in high relief (Fig. 7 and 8). The way of making pillow-lace (dentelles) consists in dexterous twisting and plaiting of the threads after an ingenious system. As regards the fineness of this pillow-lace there are considerable differences in its degree, which exercise the greatest influence on the difficulty of the work, as well as on its preciousness.

The lace-ornament follows closely the other Renaissance ornament, with the only restriction, that here, of course, vegetable motives prevail, without exclusion, however, of figural representations, as birds etc.

Fig. 1, 2 and 3. Venetian point lace.
  „ 4, 5 and 6. Venetian point lace in relief.
  „ 7 and 8. Do. with highly raised leaves. } Needle-made.
  „ 9. Roselina-lace.
  „ 10. Reticella-lace.
  „ 11. Italian Guipure.
  „ 12. Genoa church-lace. } Pillow-made.
  „ 13. Collar in Venetian Guipure.

CEILING PAINTING.

Printed by Max Berger, Stuttgart, Germany.

LACES.

Plate 51.

ITALIAN RENAISSANCE.

EMBROIDERY and CARPET WEAVING.

In accordance with its love of pomp and splendour, the Renaissance period did not fail to express this disposition by making skilfully embroidered robes, carpets, etc. Churches especially were richly furnished with such vestments.

Embroidery, either appliqué or flat work, the latter frequently relief-like, took its motives from the same sources as the hitherto treated branches of art, and it also united with the mere ornament proper images, especially in form of medallions.

Carpet-weaving, inasmuch as it is not fancy-weaving, but applying geometric or vegetable designs, follows in the main features Byzantine and Oriental examples.

Here also bright colours are in great favour, and especially for embroidered fabrics, gold is used everywhere, in accordance with the general inclination for ostentatious display.

Fig. 1. Embroidery on an ecclesiastical mantle in 'S. Croce at Florence'.

„ 2. Embroidered little velvet cover in the 'Museum vaterländischer Altertümer' at Stuttgart.

„ 3. Embroidered velvet-border from a chasuble, ibid.

„ 4. Silk-embroidery in appliqué work from a chasuble, ibid.

„ 5. Relief-embroidery in gold upon silk from a chasuble, ibid.

„ 6 and 7. Silk-embroideries in appliqué work upon damask-ground.

„ 8. Carpet-border from a Venetian picture at Verona.

„ 9. Do. from a picture by Paolo Giolfino in the museum, ibid.

„ 10. Do. „ „ „ by Moroni in the Pinacothec at Munich.

Plate 52.

ITALIAN RENAISSANCE.

SGRAFFITOS, WOOD-MOSAIC, MARBLE-MOSAIC AND BASSO RELIEVOS.

The sgraffito-ornament is not to be considered as a mere flat-ornament, as it shows for the most part a tendency to imitate plastic decoration by design, without however having other tones of colour at disposal, than black, white and grey, the latter being produced by hatching.

The process of making sgraffito consists in covering the surface to be decorated with dark stucco, which is afterwards white-washed with lime-water. The required designs are then produced by scraping away with iron styles, as far as required, the upper coat of white, revealing thereby the dark ground underneath. By this simple process sgraffito, in opposition to painted and inlaid ornaments, keeps more the character of a design, notwithstanding which, by a judicious distribution of light and shade, sometimes compositons of a grand and rich effect can be attained.

On the sgraffito-fronts the plastical mouldings appear only rarely, for often the very frame of the architecture is marked by means of sgraffito.

As regards ornamental flooring we meet in Renaissance art, besides the linear mosaic-ornament (as it occurs very similarly in the early Christian and middle ages) with intarsia-marbles and niello-marbles. In order to make the former, the cut-out marble pieces are inlaid in the correspondingly hollowed out ground, whereas for making niello-marbles, the deepened places are filled up with black or red stucco, or sometimes with metal. The coloration of these floor-decorations is always simply treated, whereas the designs frequently go beyond the legitimate bounds of ornament, as for instance in the cathedral at Siena, the renowned floor of which shows many-figured historical representations, sometimes together with perspective architecture.

Basso relievos are mostly made without the assistance of coloured contrasts, the ground only being made rough, above which the flatly treated ornament rises but a little.

Fig. 1. Sgraffito on a house at Rome. Via Giulia Nr. 82.
" 2. " " " " " " Via dei Coronari Nr. 148.
" 3. " " " " " " Vicolo Calabraga Nr. 31 and 32.
" 4. " " " " " " Vigna alla via Porta S. Sebastiano Nr. 27.
" 5 and 6 " " " " " " Borgo al vicolo del Campanile Nr. 4.
" 7. Inlaid marble-Work on the floor of the cathedral at Siena.
" 8 and 9. " " " from a tomb-plate in San Giovanni e Paolo at Venice.
" 10. " " " " " " " " " in Sta. Croce at Florence.
" 11. " " " " " " " " " in the Frari-church at Venice.
" 12 and 13. Basso relievos from tomb-plates in Sta. Maria del Popolo at Rome.
" 14 and 15. " " from the tomb of Vendramin in San Giovanni e Paolo at Venice.

Printed by K. Hochdanz, Stuttgart, Germany.

EMBROIDERY AND CARPET WEAVING.

SGRAFFITOS, WOOD-MOSAIC, MARBLE-MOSAIC AND BASSO RELIEVOS.

Plate 53.

ITALIAN RENAISSANCE.

CEILING ᴀɴᴅ WALL PAINTING.

Ornamental wall-and ceiling painting of High-Renaissance is represented in its highest beauty and dignity by the works of Raffaelle and his school, especially in the Loggie of the Vatican. Although a great part of those paintings are not from his own hand, yet they were carried out by his pupils after the master's designs, and in his spirit. We cannot fail to recognize however, that the Thermae of Titus, shortly before detected at Rome, exercised a great influence, especially the union of stucco with marble; but these classic examples not only instigated the master to imitation, but they incited him also to create new variations of motives for figures, garlands etc. Thus the Vatican presents to the spectator a grand richness of paintings, in which the figures and ornaments, decoration and architecture, and more particularly the colours, are balanced in the nicest proportions. — Remarkable is the prevalence of secondary colours. (Fig. 2.)

To a pupil of Raffaelle also, the paintings in the Palazzo Doria at Genoa are to be ascribed. Although they do not equal the superiority of Raffaelle's works, yet they are throughout beautiful in their details, and prove especially an eminent ingenuity in combining the colours. —

Concerning the motives employed, compare the above with plate 45 and ff.

Fig. 1. Ceiling-painting in the Palazzo Doria at Genoa.
  „ 2. Pilaster-decoration from the Loggie of the Vatican at Rome.
  „ 3 and 4. Panels in a window-niche in the Vatican Museum, ibid.

Plate 54.

ITALIAN RENAISSANCE.

ILLUMINATION, WEAVING and MARBLE-MOSAIC.

The invention of the art of printing was of the most important consequence for the illumination of manuscripts. For in proportion as the multiplication of literary productions became easier and simpler and hence their market-price considerably cheaper, so much less labour was bestowed upon the artistic decoration by painting, particularly since the new art offered also the means of producing beautiful initials and title pages. Notwithstanding we find, even at that time, many artists occupied in illumination; for in the period of Renaissance the printing of books did not embrace all branches of literature, and even in printed books a title executed by hand, or initials sigularly decorated, especially with different colours, were still favoured by the public. Therefore that period gives us still many examples of fine illumination, presenting frequently a varied mixture of antique, mythological and Christian motives. The vegetable arabesques of the initials, as well as the leaves and flowers, show us fewer natural than conventionally idealised forms.

However, decidedly natural are these forms in the most carefully (and with infinite diligence) executed mosaics, composed of smaller and larger marble pieces of the mostvarious colours. With such decorations table-slabs, chests etc. were embellished, and at Florence this technique is still cultivated with success up to the present day.

The greatest affinity with the traditional ornament is manifest in weaving, which, without keeping clear of modern influences, preferred going back to Oriental models. Compare Plate 51.

Fig. 1—6. Paintings from divers manuscripts.
,,   7. Velvet-stuff in the 'Museum vaterländischer Altertümer' at Stuttgart.
,,   8. Border from a silk-stuff.
,,   9. Marble-mosaic from a table in the National Museum at Munich.

Printed by Max Seeger, Stuttgart, Germany.

CEILING- AND WALL-PAINTING.

ILLUMINATION, WEAVING AND MARBLE-MOSAIC.

Printed by E. Hochdanz, Stuttgart, Germany

Plate 55.

ITALIAN RENAISSANCE.

POTTERY PAINTING.

The earthenware called 'majolica' in all probability derives its name from the island of Majorca, where glazed pottery was extensively manufactured, especially by the Moors, and whence this art found its way into Italy. In our days the term 'majolica' is generally applied to all finer fayence-ware, when executed with more care than coarser pottery i. e. to such earthenware, the mains substance of which is potter's clay covered with nontransparent glaze, and coloured. There were two ways of glazing pottery: either the vessel of clay (terra-cotta) after having received the required shape, was burnt, then plunged into a fluid not transparent, tin-glazing and immediatly afterwards painted, then finally burnt again, or, since the mentioned process remained for a long time the secret of single masters, one chose the following way: the rude earthen object was covered with a thin layer of white pipe-clay, and only after that the transparent lead-glazing was put on.

Tin-glazing is believed to have been invented by Lucca della Robbia, who towards the close of the 15th century effected thereby a total change in the fayence-technique. The numerous splendid reliefs created by members of this artist's family attained high celebrity.

Up to the present day, the Italian majolicas of the Renaissance period excite our well-deserved admiration, not only on account of the noble forms of the various. vessels, but chiefly for the paintings they are covered with. Those clay-formers and clay-painters were masters of their branch, and although the ready sale of their productions induced many of them to manufacture rather mechanically, yet all these objects manifest a fine feeling of artistic form and sublime beauty.

As regards the colours used, blue, green, yellow, orange and violet prevail, as already above said. Many vessels exhibit a rich pearly lustre, other pieces a comparatively rare red and other colours, marks which point to a certain master, or a certain manufactory.

On these dishes, plates, etc. not only scroll work, single figures, etc. were represented, but even copies or free transformations of whole images and pictures by famous masters, frequently and in preference so that these pictorial representations covered the whole vessel, the borders of the dishes etc.

Fig.   1. Lower termination of a Madonna-relief by the Robbia-school.
  „   2. Surface-pattern on the vestry-fountain in the church St. Maria novella at Florence.
  „   3—5. Border-decorations on dishes from the manufactory at Faenza.
  „   i 6. Belly-decoration on a handled vase from the same.
  „   7—9. Profile-decorations on a vase from the same.
  „   10. Profile-decoration on an inkstand from the same.
  „ 11—13. Border-decorations on dishes from the same.
  „ 14—19. Do on dishes from the manufactory at Chaffagiolo.
  „   20.   „   „   „   „   „   „   „ Gubbio.
  „ 21—23. „   „ . „   „   „   „   „ Urbino.
  „ 24—27. Divers vessels from the manufactory at Urbino.
  „   28. Dish from the manufactory at Pesaro.
  „   29. Border-decoration on a dish from the manufactory at Pesaro.

Plate 56.

ITALIAN RENAISSANCE.

PLASTIC ORNAMENTS in MARBLE und BRONZE.

Marble-sculpture revived with a vigour never known in former times. There exists this difference between High Renaissance and Early Renaissance, that the former liked strong intersections of the flower and scroll-work as well as of the figural element. The capitals show, especially in Early Renaissance a close affinity with those of the Corinthian ordre; but the volutes are now frequently replaced by vegetable motives, mostly however by dolphins, dragons, cornucopiae etc. In this very point the eminent productivity of the Renaissance manifests itself principally. Also figural adornment of the capitals is not wanting. The acanthus-leaf however appears more scantily, usually only in one row. With High Renaissance begins then a time, where the artists more closely followed the antique orders, which all revive in this period.

Fig. 9.

It was the bronze-technique which in point of modelling overstepped nearly all limits, the consequence of which wa as direct imitation of nature, especially in the vegetable ornament.

How the flourishing of art influenced even common objects in a high degree, is shown by the two fine door-knockers.

Fig.   1. Door-lintel with marble-frieze in the Palazzo Ducale at Urbino. XV. century.

    „   2. Frieze on a marble-chimney ibid.

    „   3. Console-capital of marble from the church Fonte Giusta at Siena. XV. cent. (close).

    „   4. Frieze on a tomb.

    „   5. Door-frame of bronze from the Ghiberti Gate of the Baptistery at Florence.

    „   6. Panel of a pilaster-strip in marble from the altar in the church Fonte Giusta at Siena.

    „ 7 and 8. Door-knockers of bronze.

    „   9. Capital of a column from the portal of the Badia at Florence.

NEC SPE
NEC METV

Printed by E. Hochdanz, Stuttgart, Germany.

POTTERY PAINTING.

Printed by Max Seeger Stuttgart, Germany.

PLASTIC ORNAMENTS IN MARBLE AND BRONZE.

Plate 58.

ITALIAN RENAISSANCE.

WORKS IN PRECIOUS METALS WITH PAINTINGS IN ENAMEL.

The works in precious metals comprise two kinds: on the one side those objects, which, being made of precious metals, were still decorated in a particular manner with precious stones, pearls and enamel (for instance jewelry); on the other those by which any rare mineral, such as lapis lazuli, onyx, etc., or a beautifully formed glass were made into a vessel or utensil of luxury, by the application of a handle, foot, cover etc. For both kinds, Benvenuto Cellini was the leading master about the middle of the 16th century.

The colours chosen are harmoniously combined. The noble vessels, especially their handles and lids, gave ample opportunity to represent a profusion of elegant lines and beautiful forms. Plants, animals, human figures, frequently in the most strange compositions, by far preponderate over the purely geometric ornament.

On the whole French Renaissance follows in metal-work of this kind, at least during the 16th century, the Italian style, for it was by Italian artists, that the new style was introduced into France. The change proceeded slowly, of course, in the native country of the Gothic style, which accounts for the fact that many features of the pointed art remained, or that the artists who had divested themselves of the latter, fell into a rather arbitrary practise.

Printed by E. Hochdanz, Stuttgart, Germany.

CEILING- AND WALL-PAINTING.

Printed by E. Hochdanz, Stuttgart, Germany.

WORKS IN PRECIOUS METALS WITT PAINTINGS IN ENAMEL.

Plate 59.

FRENCH RENAISSANCE.

TYPOGRAPHIC ORNAMENTS.

Already towards the end of the 15th century, French printers, especially at Paris and Lyon, were highly renowned for the carefulness and beauty of their prints. Yet they had not their own ways in forming initials, flourishes etc., until Tory, so well deserved of French book-ornamentation, released his countrymen from their slavish dependence on Italian models, by offering them original decorations of his own invention. They still clung for a long time, far into the 16th century, to the Gothic forms; even when the nobility of France had been made acquainted with the Italian renaissance by travelling or by foreign artists, still the firm attachment to the old style impeded the development of a specific French renaissance ornament so much, that Italian (and German) examples prevailed almost throughout (Fig. 1). Then, about 1520, that change was inaugurated by Tory. His ornaments, consisting mainly of flowers and foliage, sometimes united with figural representations, are simple lines, in initials for the most part, white on black ground (Fig. 2) and not shaded. In this method he follows the Italian custom. — His mode of representation and his forms survived him for a long time.

Nevertheless Italy continued to exercise a certain amount of influence, a proof of which we have in the "puttini", or chubby boys, as well as in initials directly borrowed from Italian masters (Fig. 14).

The graceful elegance of the French renaissance ornament is especially obvious in Figs. 9—11, where however we are reminded of Arabian ornaments, as in Fig. 2 of Gothic ones. Figs. 6 and 12 show acanthus elegantly applied.

Fig. 4 exhibits the manner in which titles of books or whole pages were decorated.

Fig. 1. Initial from the time of Louis XII. by Tory.
" 2. " " " " " François I. " "
" 3. " " " " " " " " Claude Garamont.
" 4. Cartouche from the time of Henri II. by Jean Goujon.
" 5. Initial " " " " " " " "
" 6. " " " " " " " from Salomon Bernard's school.
" 7 and 8. Initials " " " " " " " " " "
" 9—11. Borders " " " " " " by Petit Bernard.
" 12. Initial " " " " " III. " John Tornesius.
" 13. " " " " " " IV.
" 14. " " " " " Louis XIII.
" 15. Tail-piece " " " " " "

Fig. 15.

Plate 60.

FRENCH RENAISSANCE.

BLOCK PRINTING AND EMBROIDERY.

With the term "block printing" we designate the printing or stamping of a certain repeated pattern on stuff. In Fig. 1, 2, 4 the design is raised like high-relief, whilst in Fig. 3 the outlines project but little above the ground.

The rather hard treatment of the acanthus leaf in Figs. 1 and 4, the arbitrary arrangement of the decoration in Fig. 1 and the super-abundance in Fig. 1—3 demonstrate at once the later origin of these designs, whilst the simple and, when compared with the other ornaments, noble treatment of the embroidery betrays much more the connexion with the antique.

Fig. 1, 2 and 4. Patterns in relief-printing, XVII. century.

„ 3. Pattern in flat printing, XVII. century.

„ 5. Border on an embroidered carpet in the Musée du Louvre, XVI. cent. The ground-pattern of this carpet follows in Plate 64.

In all these Figures yellow means gold. In Fig. 3 the original has grey-violet instead of red.

Printed by Max Seeger, Stuttgart, Germany.

TYPOGRAPHIC ORNAMENTS.

Printed by K. Hochdanz, Stuttgart, Germany.

BLOCK PRINTING AND EMBROIDERY.

Plate 61.

FRENCH RENAISSANCE.

CARPET PAINTING.

The carpet-like painting of dwelling-rooms, so much favoured in the Gothic period, was carried forward into the Renaissance. But even here, notwithstanding a frequent going back to antique forms, the Gothic tradition breaks out very often, or Oriental influences impede the development of a pure renaissance.

Usually the painting was done in such way, that about the two lower thirds of the walls were covered with a fuller and heavier pattern, the upper portion with a simpler and lighter one (compare Fig. 3 and 4). Scroll-work, where it occurs, is nearly always much idealised; the paraphs (initials) of the sovereigns as well as crowns, and the lily, (the royal insignia of France), recur most frequently in this ornament. — Regarding coloration the secondary and tertiary colours are in favour; gold is frequently used.

Fig. 1—9. Painted carpet-patterns in the Castle at Blois from the time of François I.

(By mistake Fig. 6 was drawn upside down.)

Plate 62.

FRENCH RENAISSANCE.

PLASTIC ORNAMENTS IN STONE AND WOOD.

In sculpture French renaissance appears clearer of strange ingredients than in other departments. Especially in the first time the ornament shows a fine and noble treatment of low and high reliefs, being almost without exception mixed ornament, in which the cartouches (framed tablets) play a conspicuous part, their forms being adaptable to the most various shapes. In Early Renaissance the cartouches are still treated in a rather simple way, later on, however, they become richer and rolled up bolder on their edges. — The acanthus-leaf is in as great favour as in Italian renaissance, and treated lighter or harder according to the time.

The shafts of the pilasters and columns are richly adorned; the capitals often exhibit peculiar compositions, sometimes overloaded, it is true, but frequently by no means wanting a certain elegance.

Fig. 1. Pilaster-capital from a chimney in the Hôtel Lasbordes at Toulouse (François I.).
„ 2. Carved panel on the wainscot of the gallery of François I. in the castle at Fontainebleau.
„ 3. Carved panel-ornament from a door in the Justice-palace at Dijon (François I. till Henri II.).
„ 4. Torus-decoration in the chapel of the Castle at Anet (Henri II.).
„ 5. Decoration of a window-frame on the Louvre at Paris (Henri II.).
„ 6. Wood-rosette from the gallery of Henri II. in the Castle at Fontainebleau.
„ 7. Rosette from a chimney in the Castle at Anet (Henri II.).
„ 8. Herma from the Hôtel d'Assezat at Toulouse (Henri II.).
„ 9. Panel on a chimney in the Museum of the Hôtel de Cluny at Paris (Henri II.).
„ 10. Wood-carved panel on a door of the chapel near the Castle at Anet (Henri II.).
„ 11. Capital from the baptistery of Louis XIII. in the Castle at Fontainebleau.

Printed by K. Hochdanz, Stuttgart, Germany.

CARPET PAINTING.

Printed by Max Seeger, Stuttgart, Germany.

PLASTIC ORNAMENTS IN STONE AND WOOD.

Plate 63.

FRENCH RENAISSANCE.

CEILING-PAINTING.

In this plate span-ceilings only are taken into consideration, the character of which is entirely preserved by the applied painting. Each single beam has a special painting, several of them together forming a pattern regularly repeated (Fig. 1, 3, 5). The lateral faces of the beams have generally only one tone; the connecting beams however, are distinguished by a rich decoration on the sides and on the under face (Fig. 2, 4 and 6—8).

The vegetable ornament shows sometimes a decided going back to the antique; the figural element is also frequently employed.

Fig. 1 and 3. Painted ceilings of timbers in the Castle at Blois (François I.).
   „   2 and 4. Painted binding-beams on the same ceilings.
   „   5. Painted span-ceiling in the Castle at Wideville (Louis XIII.).
   „ 6, 7 and 8. Painted binding-beams on the same ceiling.

Plate 64.

FRENCH RENAISSANCE.

WEAVING EMBROIDERY AND BOOK-COVERS.

— ·

Great care used to be bestowed on the binding of books, according to their importance; their covers were decorated in two ways: either a continuous pattern spread over the surface of the cover, whilst only the corners were specially splendidly distinguished, a small shield in the middle being sometimes added; or the ornament constitutes a many-membered whole with tendril-work and geometric elements alternately. The small shield in the middle with the library-mark, the book-title, or the name of the owner, generally occurs here too. Fig. 4 and 5 represent the former way, Fig. 6 and 7 the latter, which however is rather too profuse. During the period of good style, the ornament in work of this kind is, almost throughout, treated as flat-ornament.

Fig. 1. Silk weaving (close of the XVII. century).
„ 2. Silk-weaving (midst of the XVI. century).
„ 3. Embroidered carpet in the Musée du Louvre (XVI. century). The border belonging to it see Plate 60, Fig. 5.
„ 4 and 5. Corner-pieces of a book-cover made of red morocco (Henry III.).
„ 6. A book-cover from the beginning of the XVII. century.
„ 7. The same from the close of the XVI. century.

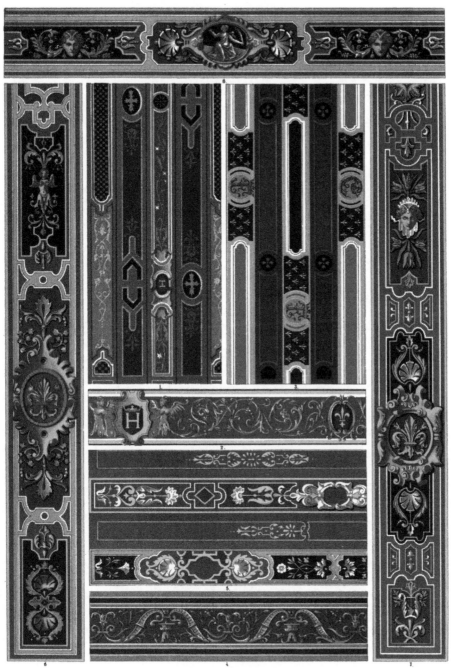

Printed by K. Hochdanz, Stuttgart, Germany.

CEILING-PAINTING.

Printed by K. Hochdanz, Stuttgart, Germany.

WEAVING, EMBROIDERY AND BOOK-COVERS.

FRENCH RENAISSANCE.

WALL-PAINTING, POLYCHROME SCULPTURE, WEAVING AND BOOK-COVERS.

On this plate the difference between Earlier and Later French Renaissance is most striking. Whereas Figs. 1 and 2 show an elegant but moderate movement. Figs. 3 and 4 even a certain rigidness of the rather hard forms, in Fig. 8 on the contrary all is activity and lively motion, the garlands themselves seeming to wave in the wind. Besides, the arrangement and combination of the single groups, as well as the excessive profusion of figural motives, point to a time when the principle of wise moderation did no longer prevail in the artistic productions. This want of fine restriction appears also in the two book-covers (Figs. 6 and 7), which exemplify another kind of decoration than the one represented on plate 64, Figs. 4—7.

In Figs. 2—5, 10 and 11 we recognize that, in painting plastic ornaments few colours were used, that however gold always predominated. In stucco-decorations the latter was often the only colour used, set off at the utmost by a coloured ground. (Compare Figs. 10 and 11.)

Fig. 1. Painted frieze on both sides of a chimney in de Hôtel d'Aluie at Blois. Style of Louis XII. (I. half of the XVI. century.)

  „ 2. Wood-carved panel from the Castle at Gaillon. Style Louis XII. (I. half of the XVI. cent.)

  „ 3 and 4. Carved and painted girder-panels on a ceiling in Assize-court at Dijon. Style of François I. (I. half of the XVI. cent.)

  „ 5. Carved and painted ceiling-panel from the Diana-chamber in the Castle at Anet. Style of Henri II. (Middle of the XVI. cent.)

  „ 6 and 7. French-book-covers. (II. half of the XVI. cent.)

  „ 8. Painted wall-panel in the library of the arsenal at Paris. Style of Henri IV. — Louis XIII. (I. half of the XVII. cent.)

  „ 9. Painted wall-frieze from the Castle at Fontainebleau. Style of Louis XIII. (I. half of the XVII. cent.)

  „ 10. and 11. Painted stucco-friezes from the Galerie d'Apollon in the Louvre at Paris (by Berain). Style of Louis XIV. (II. half of the XVII. cent.)

  „ 12. Border from a Gobelin (by le Brun). Style of Louis XIV. II. half of the XVII. cent.)

Plate 66.

FRENCH RENAISSANCE.

GOBELINS.

W̲e have pointed out before, that the windows, painted in imitation of carpets, owe their origin to the custom of covering the openings for the day-light with carpets. In course of time the wall-surfaces, treated in the same manner, in order to give them a more comfortable appearance, were likewise adorned with colours, i. e. with pictures or simple designs. Meanwhile however, the use of carpets for such purposes was not entirely dispensed with, and especially, since the 16th. century such wall-decorating carpets again found favour in the houses of the wealthy, all the more since the hangings of wool, woven in the Netherlands, and embellished with various figural representations, were sold all over the world and quite superseded the silk or linen tapestry. Also in France, under Louis XIV. such a manufactory of tapestry was established by Gobelin brothers, from whom the tapestries woven there, and afterwards all fabrics of this kind were named, 'Gobelins'.

Although this manufacture is a very difficult and troublesome one, yet a glance at our plate, shows that in point of fact this mode of painting does not either, in respect of colours or of forms, meet with invincible obstacles.

Fig. 1—3. Borders on a tapestry carpet after Le Brun (made 1665—72).
   „ 4—6. Border from a tapestry after Noel Coypel (made 1670—80).
   „ 7.   „   „   „   „   of the XVI. century.

Printed by K. Hochdanz, Stuttgart, Germany.

WALL-PAINTING, POLYCHROME SCULPTURE, WEAVING AND BOOK COVERS.

Printed by E. Hochdanz, Stuttgart, Germany.

GOBELINS.

Plate 67.

FRENCH RENAISSANCE.

ENAMEL ON METAL, POTTERY PAINTING
AND METAL-MOSAIC.

It was at Limoges that enamel-painting attained a high degree of perfection. Figs. 1—10 show us not only smaller and simpler gold-decorations, but also complicated scroll-work, even figural representations, painted in this way, the choice of colours being almost unlimited.

The difference in the productions of our period and those of the middle ages consists chiefly in the circumstance that the metal, forming the underground, was not visible. Most frequently we find enamel painted in grisaille, gold being always put on, whilst coloured representations, when required, were executed with semi-transparent vitrifiable pigments.

Figs. 11 and 12 represent two fayence gable-heads very much favoured, especially in palaces, as a finish of gables, towers etc.

Among the fayence-painters of the 16th century Bernard Palissy, of whose works we give some specimens in Figs. 13—18, was of great importance for French ornamentation. The decorations of his fayences are not flat, but consist in brilliantly coloured reliefs of a warm and vigorous tone. He brought in fashion especially those plates, on which various animals of the water, earth and air are painted with remarkable fidelity to nature. But complete pictures also owe him their origin. Finally his ornaments, executed in but few colours, are to be reckoned among the most graceful of French Renaissance.

A century and a half after Palissy another artist attained a certain celebrity at the French court, viz. André Charles Boule, cabinet-maker to King Louis XVI. He had a special skill in decorating objects of any kind with inlaid-work. From him marquetry composed of different metals, mother-of-pearl, ivory, tortoise-shell, fine woods etc. is commonly called Boule-Work. (Fig. 21.)

Fig. 1—10. Decorations on Limoges-vessels (copper-enamelling), Fig. 1 in private possession. Fig. 2 from the Galerie d'Apollon in the Louvre at Paris. Fig. 3 and 4 in the Bavarian National Museum at Munich.

„ 11 and 12. Fayence gable-heads.

„ 13—18. Decorations on fayence vessels by Bernard Palissy. From the Musée du Louvre at Paris and in private possession.

„ 19 and 20. Borders on fayence plates from Rouen.

„ 21. Little Boule-chest in the Musée du Louvre at Paris.

Plate 68.

FRENCH AND GERMAN RENAISSANCE.

ORNAMENTS ON WOOD AND METALS ETC.

The productions of the artisans of that period have a singular charm, art taking a lively part in the decoration of manufactures. We see arms, little chests, articles of every-day-life etc., most variously ornamented, either by inlaying of ivory etc., when they are made of wood, or mostly by engraving and etching when made of metal.

To Fig. 18—21 may be observed, that the so-called fayences (named also Henri-Deux-ware) from the approximate time of their origin derive their name from a French castle, where this earthenware was made during the first half of the 16th century. Its pecularity is, that the ornaments and figures are traced on the surface, as in niello, the ground probably having been deepened according to circumstances either by a mould or by an instrument, whereupon the deepenings were filled up with a mass mostly yellow and brown coloured.

Fig. 1. Boule work from a clock in the "Museum vaterländischer Altertümer" at Stuttgart (French).

„ 2 and 3. Inlaid wood work of ebony and ivory from a table ibid. (German).

„ 4. Inlaid wood work from a tent-bed in the golden hall at Urach (German).

„ 5 and 6. Inlaid wood work on a wall-deepening in the palace of justice at Dijon (French).

„ 7. Inlaid wood work from a chest at Ravensburg (German).

„ 8. Silver inlaid work on a golden bumper in the Royal treasury at Munich (German).

„ 9. Inlaid ivory work on a pistol in the Royal Historical Museum at Dresden (German).

„ 10. Low relief from a tent-bed in the golden hall at Urach (German).

„ 11. Do. from a wooden frame with gilt ground in the Musée de Cluny at Paris (French).

„ 12. Motive for etched or engraved work by Peter Flötner (German).

„ 13. Iron etched work on a padlock from the Collegiate Church Heiligenkreuz in the "K. K. österr. Museum f. K. und I." at Vienna (German).

„ 14. Iron etched work on a saw in the Royal Historical Museum at Dresden (German).

„ 15 and 16. Small borders on the cover of a little gilt silver chest, by Wenzel Jamnitzer in the Royal treasury at Munich (German).

„ 17. Motive for etched or engraved work (unknown German master).

„ 18 and 19. Small borders on Oiron vessels in the Musée du Louvre at Paris (French).

„ 20 and 21. Surface patterns on Oiron vessels ibid. (French).

Printed by E. Hochdanz, Stuttgart, Germany.

ENAMEL ON METAL, POTTERY PAINTING AND METAL-MOSAIC.

Printed by K. Hochdanz, Stuttgart, Germany.

ORNAMENTS ON WOOD AND METALS ETC.

Plate 69.

GERMAN RENAISSANCE.

CEILING and WALL-PAINTING, WOOD-MOSAIC and EMBROIDERY.

Although German Renaissance, taking its own way, deviates still more from the antique than Italian and French did, yet there are always traces, (and often very clear ones), visible, which lead back to the mother-land of Renaissance. Figs. 2—5, for instance, show unquestionably Italian influence, which however may easily be explained by the fact, that the authors of those paintings travelled to Italy to study there. So amongst others, A. D ü r e r took a longer sojourn in Italy to become acquainted with the new style in its birth-place. —

In these paintings generally light and gay tones are chosen upon an entirely or nearly uncoloured ground, their character bearing much resemblance to old Roman decorations. The same is to be said of Fig. 1. Probably the author of these and other similar decorations in the Fugger-house was an Italian master, called by the rich Fugger from Italy according to the custom of that time, and charged with decorating his grandly built house.

Fig. 6 gives a specimen of that inlaid-work so frequently found, which commands the just admiration of our time by the charming designs as well as the exquisite elegance of the ornaments, by the inexhaustible variety of motives and the amazing patience and labour bestowed upon it. In these objects too, the artists set a high value on effective coloring, the shades being burnt in.

In the middle portion of this figure we observe a form of ornamentation peculiar to German Renaissance and deriving its origin no doubt, from the art of smithing which then was most flourishing; for we see flat metal-work with its rivets and nails directly imitated, and the bands, into which the imitated sheet-metal runs out, frequently elaborated into idealised foliage, or curved and rolled up.

Concerning linen embroidery, it is not unknown how carefully it was fostered in the German family. Great artists themselves, such as H o l b e i n father and son, did not disdain to support this branch of art-industry by designs of their own hands.

Fig. 1. Wall-painting from the bath-rooms in the Fugger-house at Augsburg.
  „ 2, 3 and 5. Do. in the knights' hall of the Trausnitz at Landshut.
  „ 4. Ceiling-painting ibid.
  „ 6. Wood inlaid work from the cover of a little chest.
  „ 7. Embroidered border on a linen cover.

Plate 70.

GERMAN RENAISSANCE.

STAINED GLASS PAINTING.

Glass-painting is to a certain degree an exception from the general flourish of art-industry during the time of Renaissance. Although in town-halls and guild-rooms, in the castles of the nobility and the houses of citizens glass-panes painted with coats of arms, symbolical or historical representations etc., were often found, and as a rule beautifully executed, yet this art vanishes more and more from the sphere most favourable to its development, viz. the erection of churches; later on, however, the glass-painters, sedulously striving to get the start of painting proper, were misled into great figural compositions, which are, strictly speaking, quite opposed to the true principles of this art.

However it still confines itself to its limits i. e. in the glass-paintings of the Chapel in the Royal residence at Munich. Serving principally for decorative purposes, they are of great beauty in spite of a certain tendency towards naturalism.

Figs. 1—3. Glass-paintings from the dome of the rich Chapel in the Royal residence at Munich.

Printed by K. Hochdanz, Stuttgart, Germany.

CEILING AND WALL-PAINTING, WOOD-MOSAIC AND EMBROIDERY.

Printed by E. Hochdanz, Stuttgart, Germany.

STAINED GLASS PAINTING.

Plate 71.

GERMAN RENAISSANCE.

METAL-WORK.

———

Our entire plate is devoted to one special branch of metal-work embracing such numerous objects, viz. productions of the armourers. Many weapons and armours, the surfaces of which are, with marvellous ingenuity and endless variety, decorated with scroll-work, frame-work and strap-work, were for this reason for a long time believed to be works of the greatest Italian masters, who were thought to have made them chiefly at the French court. Some years ago, however, the surprising discovery was made, that the most and very finest of these objects were of German origin, German masters, above all, having been called by Francis I. and Henry II. for that purpose to France.

Part of these harnesses, shields, helms etc. are most splendidly decorated with complete figural representations, others with single figures, animals, birds, mythical beings as well as with flowers and scroll-work; later on, however, the scrolls and involuted bands, likewise the cartouches predominated, as they did in Italian and French Renaissance, taking the place of that finer vegetable ornament of the former time.

The metal-plates were either etched, chased or damascened, more frequently however the designs were raised by embossment.

———

Figs. 1—6. Representations of armour from the "Kabinet der Handzeichnungen alter Meister" at Munich.

Plate 72.

GERMAN RENAISSANCE.

POLYCHROME PLASTIC WORK.

I t was the delight taken in bright, life-like representations, which induced the artists of the Renaissance period to enliven their sculpture by means of colours. The large magnificent ceiling, for instance, in the knights'-hall of the Castle at Heiligenberg is almost entirely covered with colours, which being in perfect harmony with each other, only serve to heighten the effect of the sculpture. In like manner by colouring, a peculiar charm is bestowed upon the two supporters of stags-horns and on the central figure, which wood or stone work alone would not have given them.

In wood and stone carving too of the later German Renaissance a predominance of cartouches and band-work is perceptible, the latter causing various and interesting twistings and interlacings.

The female figure in Fig. 11 represents Ursula, by birth Countess Palatine by Rhine, consort of Duke Lewis, the builder of the "Lusthaus". In the "Lusthaus" however, which unfortunately exists no more, another figure stood on the represented console, the coat of arms referring to that.

At one time about 50 such console-figures decorated the arcades surrounding those gorgeous buildings.

Figs. 1—10. Portions of the painted wood ceiling in the knights'-hall of the Castle at Heiligenberg.
„ 11. Console-figure from the arcades of the former "Lusthaus" at Stuttgart.
„ 12 and 13. Scutcheons carved from peartree-wood in the "Museum vaterländischer Altertümer" at the same place, being part of the former furniture of a hunting-chamber belonging to the family Besserer at Ulm. Carved stags-heads with rare attires are fixed in the oval nombrils.

Printed by E. Hochdanz, Stuttgart, Germany.

METAL-WORK.

Printed by E. Hochdanz, Stuttgart, Germany.

Plate 73.

GERMAN RENAISSANCE.

ORNAMENTS FOR BOOK COVERS.

———

For book-covers, the ornaments of which were, during the period of good style, always treated as flat-ornaments, leather used to be employed almost exclusively. At first the contours of the design were sharply cut into the leather and the space, not covered by it, was deepened. Later on, however, small metal stamps were used, the patterns of which, when repeated side by side, produced the border framing the cover. In this case the corners were not specially elaborated, the borders meeting at these points by no rule. — Sometimes the book-cover is edged by such borders in several rows, an exceeding tallness of the empty central field being avoided by inserting special travers-borders along the narrow sides. The latter end was sometimes attained by beating or impressing the stamp-patterns in double rows, symmetrical to each other (Figs. 5 and 35). The central fields, being for the most part small, are then decorated either with stuff-patterns or with corner- and middle-pieces (Figs. 9—11, 13, 14, 23—26, 28—32 show patterns of the latter kind).

Besides these, however, many book-covers are found with free, often coloured arabesques and intertwisted bands (compare Plate 65, Figs. 6 and 7), these being in the flourishing time of art, framed with borders, whilst later on, instead of these borders, corner-pieces very similar to metal-work, used to be added.

The most sumptuous, of course, were covers decorated with real metal-work, especially when precious metals were employed. In this case the ornament is usually cast in relief or embossed. Fig. 1 however shows an ornament of silver simply sawn out and afterwards engraved.

Finally, may be mentioned, that in decorating the back of the book, cording in a pretty manner was made use of, this being marked either by leather pads or by deepened horizontal lines, thus producing several compartments which were filled up with simple decorations.

———

Fig. 1. Silver-eged book-cover (natural size) from the "Sammlung vaterländischer Altertümer" at Stuttgart.
„ 2 - 36. Decorations on hog's-leather covers (executed in blind-printing) from the Royal "Hand-bibliothek" at Stuttgart.

Plate 74.

GERMAN RENAISSANCE.

EMBROIDERY AND WEAVING.

Fig. 7.

In embroidery the character of the ornament depends principally, of course, on the technical process; regarding our plate, however, the immense difference between Figs. 3 and 4 on the one side and Figs. 1 and 5 on the other, results from the circumstance, that the former figures betray a strong Gothic influence, whilst in the latter the artist followed rather Oriental examples. Especially the elegant interlacing in Fig. 5, as well as the beautiful manner, in which the surfaces in Figs. 1 and 5 are filled up, recall Eastern ornaments to the beholder's mind; the weaving in Fig. 7 decidedly bearing the stamp of a marked affinity with Persian style.

But notwithstanding all that, Renaissance preserves in these patterns its peculiar nature and its original features, (Figs. 1, 5, 6.)

The embroidery in Fig. 5 was executed in the first years of the 17th century, at which time the silk-embroiderers of Munich were far and wide renowned.

Fig. 1. Table-cover embroidered in cross-stitch, in the possession of Mr. Schauffele, confectioner at Schwäbisch-Hall.
„ 2. Linen-embroidery from the Bavarian "National-Museum" at Munich.
„ 3. Embroidered border from a carpet ibid.
„ 4. Carpet embroidered on cloth. Ibid. (1560—1590.)
„ 5. Curtain-border embroidered on velvet in appliqué-work (16cm wide) from the rich chape in the Royal Residence at Munich.
„ 6. Border of a gold-embroidered leather-pouch in the Bavarian 'National-Museum' at Munich.
„ 7. Pattern of a woven material in the church at Weingarten.

Printed by K. Hochdanz, Stuttgart, Germany.

ORNAMENTS FOR BOOK COVERS.

Printed by K. Hochdanz, Stuttgart, Germany.

EMBROIDERY AND WEAVING.

Plate 75.

GERMAN RENAISSANCE.

TYPOGRAPHIC ORNAMENTS.

Fig. 14.

The custom of decorating printings with artistic initials, marginal borders etc. is nearly as old as typography itself. In the beginning, Gothic forms, of course, were still prevailing; but the transition from the 15th to the 16th century marked a new era for this branch of art. Of marked and decisive importance was particularly the activity of the greatest German artists of that period, viz of Holbein, Dürer and others; they were continually creating new ornamental alphabets and drawing titles, tail-pieces etc. thus elevating typography to a very high standard. — Numerous towns were renowned for their printing-offices, and in the third decennium of the 16th century, when the great masters were deceased, their successors could still live a long time from the store accumulated by those predecessors. However it could not fail, that in the course of time this branch also participated in the general decline of revived classical art, and Fig. 15 may prove, to what abuses wood-cut ornamentation had come down.

A glance at Plate 59 shows, that German book-ornamentation can well stand comparison with French, although the former often appears somewhat less refined than the latter.

Fig. 1. Title-frame (1519) probably by Hieronymus Hopfer.
  „ 2. Initial by A. Dürer.
  „ 3. Frieze (1539) by A. Aldengrever.
  „ 4. Initial from a dance-of-death alphabet by Hans Holbein.
  „ 5. Marginal decoration from the prayer-book of the Emperor Charles V. by A. Dürer.
  „ 6. Frieze (1528) by H. S. Beham.
  „ 7. Initial (1518) by an unknown master.
  „ 8. Do. by Paul Frank.
  „ 9. Do. by Jost Aman.
  „ 10. Do. (1527—1532) from Hans Holbein's children's alphabet.
  „ 11. Do. by an unknown master.
  „ 12. Frieze by J. Binck.
  „ 13. Initial by P. Frank.
  „ 14. Head-piece by Theodor de Bry.
  „ 15. Tail-piece by J. H. von Bemmel.

Fig. 15.

Plate 76.

GERMAN RENAISSANCE.

POLYCHROME PLASTIC WORKS.

———

O ur representations illustrate further details of the ceiling in the large knight's hall of the castle of Heiligenberg mentioned with Plate 72. This ceiling is carved entirely of lime-wood and profusely coloured, specially
with blue, red, green, gold and silver. But in spite of this richness of colours and the surprising variety
of foliage, tendrils, ribbon-work, figures etc. it does not in the least appear overladen or unquiet, but the
total impression on the eye is, as mentioned before, throughout agreeable and harmonious.

TYPOGRAPHIC ORNAMENTS.

Printed by Max Seeger Stuttgart, Germany

POLYCHROME PLASTIC WORKS.

Plate 77.

GERMAN RENAISSANCE.

PLASTIC ORNAMENTS in STONE and WOOD.

In defining the general difference between the Italian Renaissance ornament and the German, we may say, that the former, though equally profuse in the variety of forms, is still superior to the latter in refinement and elegance, especially of the figural element, and not less in a fairer distribution of the decorations over the surfaces; but there is no denying, that many achievements of German art are equivalent to those of that southern country, of which the ornamental decorations of the numerous magnificent Renaissance buildings in Germany give plain evidence.

Fig. 1. Herma from the tombs of Wurttembergian princes in the choir of the "Stiftskirche" at Stuttgart.

„ 2. Panel on the pillar of a bar in the great hall of the town-house at Nuremberg.

„ 3. Intrado on a door in the, "Otto-Heinrichs-Bau" of Heidelberg Castle.

„ 4. Dado at a tomb of the "Schenken" at Limpurg in the choir of the principal church at Gaildorf.

„ 5—10. Wood carved panels and friezes from a hall ceiling in the castle at Jever.

Plate 78.

GERMAN RENAISSANCE.

CEILING and WALL PAINTING.

O̲ur plate presents a splendid, though very peculiar mode of wall painting. The so-called golden hall in the Castle at Urach is entirely decorated in this manner. The walls are generally flat, but divided in compartments by the painting, showing throughout a decoration which involuntarily reminds the beholder of models of the iron work technique. This resemblance is all the more apparent from the various interlacements and borderings. In the latter we find the palm tree with the device "Attempto" (see Fig. 5) frequently repeated, which seems to point to the reign of "Eberhard im Bart", but the painting and architecture of the hall belong most undoubtedly to the end of the 16th century. The visible beams of the simply decorated ceiling are brownish red, but the narrow compartments between them are lightly coloured. Although the painting is limited to few colours (brownish red, white, gold and blue), yet it makes a beautiful and agreeable impression.

Fig. 1. Spandril on wall compartments.
„   2. Panel in a window flanning.
„   3 and 4. Decorations of columns.
„   5. Decoration on the window parapets.
„   6 and 7. Middle and corner pieces at the friezes bordering the wall compartments.
„   8—11. Decoration on the ceiling beams with relief wood rosettes and knos.
„   12. Wooden hood moulding.

The whole from the golden hall at Urach.

Printed by Max Seeger Stuttgart, Germany

PLASTIC ORNAMENTS IN STONE.

Printed by K. Hochdanz, Stuttgart, Germany.

CEILING AND WALL PAINTING.

Table 78 A.

GERMAN RENAISSANCE.

WALL-PAINTING, PLASTIC ORNAMENT in STONE and WOOD.

W hereas the Italian influence is distinctly shown in the German wall-painting on Pl. 69, the examples on this plate present a strong contrast to them, and we find in this cartouche-like frame-work with its bold, fanciful volutes and elegant festoons the severity peculiar to German decoration from the commencement of the XVIIth century. In German ecclesiastical Art the Gothic style was adhered to until far into the XVIth century, and only in the latter half of this century was it displaced by the Renaissance in Church architecture. However, the groined ceilings with their gorgeous keystones, the pointed and sometimes traceried windows still recall the Art of the Middle-Ages. The decorative artist by remarkable elaboration of detail then endeavoured to produce an impression of vivid colours and rich gold, recalling mediaeval colour decoration, but at the same time by the invention of new forms to create novel and charming effects. These we experience on looking at the interior of the celebrated Church at Freudenstadt, built by the Ducal Architect Heinrich Schickhardt, of Herrenberg, and the examples on our plate are sufficient witness of its rich and magnificent decoration. In the detail of this splendid composition by the painter Jakob Zuberlein we observe a capricious and rather wild imagination, as is met with, to a still greater extent in Wendel Dietterleins designs (Fig. 9), but when we see how agreeable and harmonious is the impression produced by the rich colouring of the decoration and details, we cannot but pay high respect to this period of Art, the more so as at that time the aim in the decoration of Protestant churches was to break with the old traditions, and to create new forms on entirely rational principles — an experiment which was attended with marked success in the Church at Freudenstadt.

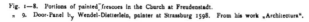

Fig. 1—8. Portions of painted frescoes in the Church at Freudenstadt.
„ 9. Door-Panel by Wendel-Dietterlein, painter at Strassburg 1598. From his work „Architectura".

Fig. 9.

WALL-PAINTING, PLASTIC ORNAMENT IN STONE AND WOOD.

Plate 79.

GERMAN RENAISSANCE.

CARTOUCHES and WORKS IN PRECIOUS METALS with ENAMEL.

The forms of German and Italian Renaissance show the greatest affinity with each other in the department of works of precious metals; for the new style was introduced into Germany mainly by such works; the German artists, on the other hand, managed to attain the standard of the Italian goldsmiths' productions not only in regarding their technical perfection, but also of the beauty of their forms. Southern Germany especially with its numerous industrial towns, soon became a centre for noted workmen in precious metals. Drinking vessels, table-services, weapons, rings, girdles, ornamented pendants, bracelets, ecclesiastical plate, etc. gave abundant scope for rich artistic treatment. However it must be mentioned, that the tendency to direct imitation of nature, especially in flowers and tendrils, as well as the liking for peculiarities soon paved the way, in this as in other departments of art, for the Baroque style.

How much cartouches were favoured in that period, we infer from their application to the most various purposes. (Figs. 1 and 2.)

Fig. 1 and 2. Cartouches from a pedigree in the "Sammlung vaterländischer Altertümer" at Stuttgart.

„ 3—17. Divers decorations on little altars, reliquaries and on a cross from the treasure of the rich chapel of the Royal Residence at Munich.

„ 18—20. Parts of ornamental objects.

„ 21—23. Parts of mountings on a baldrick after parchment drawings by Hans Mielich.

„ 24. Ornamental pendant from the "Sammlung des grünen Gewölbes" at Dresden.

„ 25. Point of a scabbard by Hans Mielich.

„ 26. Ornamental pendant from the Museum at Pest.

Plate 80.

XVII. AND XVIII. CENTURIES.

EMBROIDERY, LEATHER TAPESTRY AND GOLDSMITH'S WORK.

On our plate, the period of decaying Renaissance and the dominion of the succeeding Rococo and Baroquestyles are distinctly characterized by the naturalism of the flowers, the intricate lines, the unquiet motion in the drawing and embroidering in Fig. 1, as well as more particularly by the tendency for a plastical treatment of the ornament.

Fig. 3 belongs to the actual Rococo time.

Fig. 1. Embroidery from the "Sammlung vaterländischer Altertümer" at Stuttgart, having formerly served as a hanging over an altar in the convent church at Weingarten.

„ 2. Embroidered chasuble from the same collection.

„ 3. Border of stamped leather hangings.

„ 4 and 5. Decorations on the belly of a silver drinking cup, partly gilt, from a reproduction of the Hungarian "Landes-Kunstgewerbe-Museum" at Budapest.

Printed by Max Seeger, Stuttgart, Germany.

FRAMES AND WORKS IN PRECIOUS METALS WITH ENAMEL.

Table 80 A.

XVIIth. AND XVIIIth. CENTURIES.

GOBELIN TAPESTRY AND BOOK-BINDING.

To supplement Plate 69 we give here (Fig. 1) a Gobelin carpet with landscape back-ground, which was intended for the decoration of a salon at the palace of St. Germain.

In this fine work we admire the imaginative composition in which the decorative forms of architecture and plants, with naturalistic flowers, surround a delicately coloured landscape. The Artist responsible for this design was the painter D'Espouy, employed by Louis XIV., and he, like all great French decorators of that period, conformed to the laws and claims imposed by the technic of Gobelin weaving.

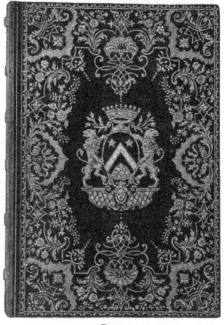

Although the preparation of the weaved copy demands great skill, and for an exact resemblance of the original a masterhand is necessary, which can employ the most effectual methods, yet we must also remember that the perfection of this »picture-weaving« absolutely depends on the excellence of the painting. At the same time the painter must keep in mind the necessity of suiting his design to the technical processes at the weaver's command, and must avoid effects only attainable by painting in oils. If these rules are followed the copied fabric will have an artistic value in spite of all temporary changes of taste.

Already at the beginning of the XVIIth. century the most celebrated artists did not disdain to place their talent in the service of the first workshop established under Henry IV., and afterwards in the royal manufactory. The French Government even succeeded in gaining for its manufacture the greatest foreign artists.

The beautiful binding from the time of Louis XV. reminds us of the forms of textile work.

Fig. 3.

Fig. 1. Gobelin tapestry for the Castle of St. Germain, designed for Louis XIV. by D'Espouy.
„ 2. Border of a gobelin carpet representing the triumph of Hercules for Louis XIV. rooms at Versailles, designed by Noël Coypel (compare Pl. 66.)
„ 3. Binding with the Arms of Gaspard Moïse de Fontanieu (1755).

Fig. 1 & 2. Drawn by N. Vivien of Paris.
„ 3. From Blanc's „Grammaire des Arts Décoratifs".

XVIIᵗʰ· AND XVIIIᵗʰ· CENTURIES.

METALWORK ᴀɴᴅ WOODCARVING.

Fig. 13.

The Baroque style, which originated in the reign of Louis XIV. first took the form of a development of the Renaissance, but appropriated to itself many characteristics of ancient work. On the whole, especially as regards ornament, it can be described as grand and noble, and is not wanting in variety and change; it suffers, however, from extravagant profusion, even to heaviness.

In the last 25 years of this reign, i. e. from 1690, the time of Charles Lebrun, the renowned decorator, there began a certain transformation in this style. The king, weary of the great ceremonials, retired into close family life, while the great banquets at Versailles were discontinued, and commissions for extensive decorative works kept on decreasing. In this way the demand arose for a less ornate and formal style, better adapted to domestic life.

Hardouin Mansart tried to bring about a revulsion in this direction, but the change was only clearly felt under Robert de Cotte, 1699, and from this point a lighter and freer form of ornament is noticeable. For further information see Pl. 82.

Fig. 1—7.   Table mountings in the Royal Bavarian Museum, Munich. (Louis XIV. Period).

„ 8—12.   Various French woodcarvings, Fig. 11 from the Choirstalls of Notredame at Paris.

„ 13.   From an Engraving.

Printed by Max Seeger, Stuttgart, Germany.

GOBELIN-TAPESTRY.

Printed by J. Schober, Karlsruhe, Germany.

METALWORK AND WOODCARVING.

Plate 81.

XVIII. CENTURY.

MOSAIC FLOORS.

Our plate represents some floors executed in a very original manner. According to the capricious style of art which extended its dominion over all the numerous German courts during the epoch in question, we do not find so much geometric patterns applied to these inlaid floors, as rather grandly composed designs, displaying full life, and having a peculiar charm through the variously coloured woods, especially where vegetable objects are represented.

The whole of the depicted patterns were executed by Johann Georg Beyer, cabinet-maker to the Wurttembergian court at Stuttgart, for the Solitude, a chateau near Stuttgart, built by Charles, Duke of Wurttemberg, during 1763—1767. However, only a small portion of these precious floors is preserved at the present day.

The original drawings are in the possession of Mr. Beyer, joiner at Ludwigsburg, a descendant of the above named cabinet-maker.

Plate 82.

XVII. AND XVIII. CENTURIES.

PLASTIC ORNAMENTS.

A glance at the Plates 82—84 enables us to recognize plainly the characteristic difference between the "Barocque", "Rococo" and "Zopf" Styles, termed also the styles of Louis Quatorze, Louis Quinze and Louis Seize.

The Louis Quatorze style appears first as a development of Renaissance, but contains many antique motives. On the whole this style can be called gorgeous and grand, especially as regards ornament; nor is it devoid of change and variety, but sometimes degenerating into luxurious extravagance, it gets overloaded. Henceforth shell-work plays a great rôle and scroll work in the corners characterizes the borders.

All this, undergoing many exaggerations towards the close of the long reign of Louis XIV., gives a basis for developing the Rococo style, which predominated under the reign of Louis XV.

Fig. 1. Panel decorations at door and window niches in the throne room of the Castle at Fontainebleau. (Style of Louis XIV.).

„ 2. Projecting plane pattern in the panels of door and window niches in the queen's bed-chamber in the same Castle. (Style of Louis XIV.)

„ 3. Wood carving from a wainscot in the Château de Bercy. (Style of Louis XIV.)

„ 4. Capital of a mirror in the state-room of the Hôtel de Lauzun at Paris. (Style of Louis XIV.)

„ 5. Capital designed by the German Master Paul Decker. (Style of Louis XIV.)

„ 6. Capital in the Salle des Médaillons of the Palace of Versailles. (Louis XV.)

„ 7. Corner of a mirror frame in the queen's bed chamber at Versailles. (Louis XV.)

„ 8. Piece of architecture in the style of Louis XV. (After A. Rosis 1753.)

„ 9. Vignette after T. Johnsohn Carver (1761). (After A. Rosis 1753.)

Fig. 9.

Printed by E. Hochdanz, Stuttgart, Germany.

MOSAIC FLOORS.

Printed by Max Seeger, Stuttgart, Germany.

PLASTIC ORNAMENTS.

Plate 82 ^A.

XVIIIth. CENTURY.

PAINTED PLASTERWORK.

The figures of our plate, as well as figs. 2 of Pl. 83 and 6 of 82^B show the nature of the Rococo style, and the method by which it was carried out in the Ducal castle of Bruchsal.

If these examples are not distinguished by the highest elegance and grace, they are at least of characteristic design and specially interesting colouring. While in the Rococo style as a rule there is beside white but little gold, the natural portions are here very gorgeously executed, and produce a very charming impression. The richness and luxuriance of this style is best shown by the large cornices which surround the ceilings (figs. 4 and 5 of this plate and fig. 2 of 83). At the same time the ground of individual panels is kept in very light tones, and sometimes gaily painted allegorical subjects are inserted. This kind of painting, which is often over raised plaster, is carried out with such nicety that separate limbs, such as feet and arms in painted plaster, are detached and stand out from the painting without at all disturbing the harmony. The centre of the ceiling is used for hanging groups or figures, or light decoration in plaster. There is probably no more agreeable combination of Architecture, Sculpture, and Painting than in the Rococo style.

The furniture, with its quaint curves, adjoins the rich wall decorations, and seems to rival them in beautiful effect.

In direct contrast to the fine ornamental scroll work of Rococo interiors is the simplicity of the noble classical severity of the exteriors of the period.

Fig. 6.

Figs. 1—3. Portions of Carved Panelling in the Ducal Castle of Bruchsal.
   „ 4—5. Portions of Plaster Ceiling in the same room.
   „ 6.   Panel by François Boucher (1703—1770).

Fig. 1—5. Drawn by H. Eberhardt, Stuttgart.

Plate 82 B.

XVIIIth. CENTURY.

GOBELIN WEAVING.

Before proceeding to consider the Gobelin work represented on this plate, we will take a glance back at the period of Louis XIV.

The most productive and brilliant period of Gobelin manufacture was about 1660, when Colbert, the able minister of Finance, conferred on the gifted painter Lebrun the direction of the workshops erected for the furniture and decoration of the Royal Castles. Lebrun could not have succeeded in the gigantic responsibilities imposed upon him by his numerous undertakings, had he not understood, like no other, how to direct his workmen to unite their efforts to accomplish the stupendous tasks, the fulfilment of which the vain king impatiently awaited, and which were only to be surmounted by skilful division of labour. Thus we often find ten painters engaged at the same time on designs, the main ideas of which almost always came from Lebrun, and it is also noticeable that such subject as flowers, friezes, landscapes, the chase, musical instruments etc. were each treated by a specialist, without the freedom of expression in the design suffering thereby.

It is no wonder, therefore, that in the ensuing period under Louis XV. and XVI. Artists such as Watteau, Boucher, Tessier, Jacques and others should have taken up the work, or that they were certain of a triumph in the pursuit of a special department of art. For instance, if we observe the tasteful manner in which Tessier, the king's-flower painter, could group his flowers and fruit in characteristic garlands, and bouquets, we shall not hesitate to reckon him one of the finest flower-painters of the French school. The details here represented, from important works by this master, give some idea of his marked ability.

Fig. 1. Chair-seat by Louis Tessier (Louis XV.).
" 2. Basket of fruit by the same Artist (Louis XV.).
" 3. Garland " " " " (Louis XV.).
" 4. Chair-Back by Jacques (Louis XVI.).
" 5. Doorpanel by this Artist (Louis XVI.).
" 6. Portion of carved panelling in the castle of Bruchsal.

Fig. 1—5. Drawn by W. Vivien, Paris.
Fig. 6. " " H. Eberhardt, Stuttgart.

Fig. 6.

Printed by B. Hachmann, Stuttgart, Germany.

PAINTED PLASTERWORK.

Printed by Max Seeger, Stuttgart, Germany.

GOBELIN-WEAVING.

Plate 83.

XVII. AND XVIII. CENTURIES.

PAINTING, LEATHER TAPESTRY AND STUCCO ORNAMENTS.

Our Fig. 2 is best fitted for exemplifying the nature of the Rococo (style of Louis XV.). For here, as also on Plate 82, Figs. 6—8, we meet with an unbounded capriciousness in the treatment of the lines, a superabundance of flowers, scroll work and cartouches, an overloading with decorative elements, Genii and figures in general being everywhere applied, and allegories, as well as emblems, very much favoured. In particular may be noted, that the decoration goes its own way, instead being subordinate to the essential forms of the construction. However it cannot be denied, that the creations of Rococo frequently exhibit a remarkably elegant and vigorous, though peculiar and bold ornamentation. Moreover we admire in this style the harmonious co-operation of architecture, sculpture and painting, rarely found elsewhere.

Fig. 1. Stamped leather hangings in the style of Louis XIV. from the "Sammlung vaterländischer Altertümer" at Stuttgart.

„ 2. Ceiling decoration from the Castle at Bruchsal.

„ 3. Painted door panel from a manor house at Paris.

Plate 84.

XVIII. CENTURY.

PLASTIC and PAINTED ORNAMENTS.

"Zopfstyle" — this term is sometimes mistaken for Barocque, even Rococo, whilst it signifies merely the style, (certainly rather barren and stiff sometimes), which art chose under Louis XVI., in opposition as it were, to the pompous and confused style under Louis XV, by returning to the antique.

Compared with the extravagances of Rococo the quiet, strict forms of the Zopfstyle produce a feeling of satisfaction in the mind of the beholder, unless, as is often the case, repose degenerates into rigidness, and strictness into barrenness.

Fig. 1. Wood carving on a wainscot in the music room of the arsenal library at Paris (Style of Louis XV.)

„ 2 and 3. Carved pilaster from the wainscot of a saloon at Paris. (Style of Louis XVI.)

„ 4. Painted frieze from the boudoir of Queen Marie Antoinette in the Castle at Fontainebleau. (do.)

„ 5. Panel of a stucco cavetto at a ceiling of a saloon at Paris. (do.)

„ 6. Carved wall panel above a saloon door in the Hôtel de Ville at Bordeaux. (do.)

„ 7. Vignette from Berthault et Bachelier (1760). (Louis XV.)

Fig. 7.

PAINTING, LEATHER TAPESTRY AND STUCCO ORNAMENTS.

Printed by Max Seeger, Stuttgart, Germany.

PLASTIC AND PAINTED ORNAMENTS.

Plate 85.

XVII. AND XVIII. CENTURIES.

LACE WEAVING AND EMBROIDERY.

The three kinds of style, last mentioned, exerted a wide influence on the ornamentation of dwelling rooms, and especially on the decoration of all objects of clothing. Here too, marked differences may easily be discerned. In Figs. 1, 2, 5 for instance, the stricter mode of idealising, points still to a certain connexion with the Rennaissance, whilst Figs. 5 and 6 and especially Figs. 4 and 7 manifest the increasing preponderance of naturalism.

Fig. 1. Lace in the style of Louis XIV., in the possession of C. Baur, manufacturer of furniture at Biberach.

  „ 2. Embroidery on a silk waistcoat. (Louis XIV.)

  „ 3. Embroidery on a silk coat (Louis XV.) from the "Sammlung vaterländischer Altertümer" at Stuttgart.

  ., 4. Silk embroidery from a velvet waistcoat (Louis XVI.) ibid.

  „ 5. Silk texture from a chasuble. (Louis XIV.)

  „ 6. Woven silk stuff for clothes. (Louis XV.)

  ., 7. Woven stuff of silk and wool. (Louis XVI.)

Printed by Hoffmann, Stuttgart, Germany.

LACE WEAVING AND EMBROIDERY.

Plate 86.

XVIIIth CENTURY.

METAL FITTINGS.

The love of splendour common to all French sovereigns of the XVIIth and XVIIIth centuries was especially shown in the decoration of furniture, and every period had its master, who proceeded upon new lines, according to his individual taste or talent. In the reign of Louis XIV., when gigantic and luxuriously fitted rooms were in vogue, we find furniture with bold mountings of bronze, as represented on Pl. 80^B, Figs. 1—7, or the luxurious creations of Boule, the famous cabinet-maker of the court (on Pl. 67 erroneously assigned to Louis XVI.), which he manufactured from ebony with bronze fittings and fine metal inlay on a tortoiseshell ground (Pl. 67, Fig. 21 and Pl. 68, Fig. 1). This gracefully-formed and effectively coloured furniture, was, however, still more appropriate for the smaller interiors of the ensuing period (the Regency and Louis XV.). The colouring became softer, and rosewood mounted in bronze was substituted for ebony. (See Fig. 16). Here especially the great talent of Charles Cressent celebrated

Fig. 16.

as sculptor, carver, and cabinet-maker comes into play, and his versatility was so great that he could impart to his work a uniform and very unusual charm. The versatile Meissonier, previously mentioned (Pl. 83) was also a goldsmith and bronzeworker of the highest reputation. In the same way we find Jacques Caffieri, the famous sculptor, founder, and carver, at work on bronzes which he very tastefully applied to furniture, — probably in conjunction with Jean François Oëben, the court cabinet-maker.

The figures of our plate show a collection of bronze furniture mountings of the time of Louis XVI., a time in which we are accustomed to see delicate decorations of a fanciful taste. To this period belongs the ornament in which swags and ribbons, doves, quivers, torches, and all kinds of trophies, are mingled into an agreeable and symbolic whole.

Figs. 1—15. Metal mountings from casts in the collection of plaster casts in the Royal Technical Institute, Stuttgart.

Fig.   16. Desk of Louis XVI. in the Louvre.

Plate 87.

COMMENCEMENT OF THE XIX.th. CENTURY.

WALL-PAINTING AND CEILING-DECORATION.

In speaking later of the so-called Empire style, we must be understood to imply the transitional style prevailing from the close of the Louis XVI. period to the first French empire, and the Empire style coming down to 1815. Although the unsettled political condition at the end of the XVIIIth century seriously threatened to extinguish the Arts in France, yet the love of art inborn in her people sprang from the chaos of the revolution, and caused the national leaders, even at the time of greatest affliction, to found a National Museum in order to preserve for future study the finest products of the Arts of past times. By this step they preserved from destruction by the revolutionary fanatics many fine works of art which tell of the days of the overthrown monarchy.

The new republicanism was destined to find increasing expression in the realm of art, in which direction a tendency was already noticeable in the style of Louis XVI. In art the craze was now for the pure Greek and Roman styles, even to the extent of reviving the dress and customs of these countries. In this change the chief part was taken by David, the famous painter, who was closely connected with politics, and who, under the administration of Napoleon I., breaking with the old order, followed the style in which Caesar had lived. Besides David, the architect Percier, associated with his colleague Fontaine, often applied his great ability to all departments of industrial art. This new French style was so esteemed that it was soon adopted all over Europe.

Figs. 1—6. Wall and ceiling decorations from King Frederick I's work-room in the castle of Ludwigsburg.

Fig.   7. Ceiling decoration by Basoli, from a photograph.

Printed by M. Hommel & Co., Stuttgart, Germany.

METAL FITTINGS.

Printed by E. Hochdanz, Stuttgart, Germany.

WALL-PAINTING AND CEILING-DECORATION.

Plate 88.

COMMENCEMENT OF THE XIXᵗʰ· CENTURY.

GOBELIN TAPESTRY AND LACEWORK.

The chief subject on this plate (Fig. 1) bears emphatic testimony to the fact that the art of flower-painting had descended without deterioration from the time of Louis XV. and XVI., when the work of Tessier, Jacques and others had attained such excellence, down to the days of the first Empire. This fine design is by the painter Saint-Ange, who was doubtless engaged in the Gobelin manufacture, but whose name, like that of many other capable artists of the kind, is but little known, and would have been completely forgotten, had they not also occupied themselves in . preparing designs to be engraved on copper, through the publication of which their names have been preserved.

Fig. 6.

While it was customary until the end of the XVIIIth century to treat with much artistic skill the frames or borders of the tapestries, the Empire period was content with reproducing in it scenes from the time of the emperors which were almost devoid of decoration.

It is interesting to compare the form of the fruit basket in Fig. 1 with those in Figs. 2 and 4 of Pl. 82B, observing how the freedom of the age of Louis XV. changes in the following period to a more rigid and formal shape, and then takes that stiff form, ornamented with classic splendour usual in the Empire style. The position which these baskets occupy with regard to their method of fixture is also characteristic. Those of the two first periods are suspended picturesquely from light ribbons, while the later example rises sedately from the stiff Roman acanthus.

The successful colouring of this design calls for special praise, as counteracting the tendency to dull colour noticeable in many ways in the style.

With regard to the hangings and draperies so popular at the time of the first Empire, we here represent characteristic examples of the period.

Fig. 1. Panel of a Screen by Saint-Ange.
Figs. 2—5. Borders of silk and velvet with woven tassels from draperies in the Castle of Ludwigsburg.
Fig. 6. Fabric in the 'Garde-Meuble' collection at Paris. (From a photograph.)

Printed by Max Seeger, Stuttgart, Germany.

GOBELIN TAPESTRY & LACEWORK.

Plate 89.

EMPIRE-STYLE. XIXᵗʰ Century.

METAL·ORNAMENTS.

The tendency towards classical forms of art very noticeable in the style of Louis XVI, is even more evident in the period now under consideration.

Furniture chiefly made of mahogony is adorned with pretty bronze ornaments, and this gives to their somewhat stiff construction a graceful form, which fully merits admiration.

The Napoleonic wars had considerable influence on the Empire-Style, in which afterwards were to be found emblems of Victory, eagles, laurel-wreaths and such like. In consequence of the Egyptian campaign new decorative elements were adopted, as for instance the capitals of Lotus-flowers, Sphinxes, winged lions and other Egyptian figures, joined sometimes to Chinese designs.

This enthusiasme for foreign forms unfortunately led to great errors by giving furniture the appearance of heavy Egyptian monuments, for instance writing tables formed like Pyramids etc., it being a common mistake to form architectural figures and ornaments of wood as though they were of stone. But in spite of such faults we must acknowledge, that at this period many objects of industrial art were created which, even if they show a certain dryness, still please us by the really noble effect they produce.

Like in the Periods of the Styles of the preceding century, so also in the Empire-Style the new French taste very soon gained admittance in all other European countries. Owing to this circumstance the King's Palace at Stuttgart contains a very large number of the most beautiful Empire furniture, of which the greater part of the 23 illustrations on our plate has been taken.

Most interesting is the appearance of naturalistic ornamentation beside the strictly classisal Style.

Fig. 1—23. Metal-Ornaments of furniture in the King's Palace at Stuttgart and from the public collection of Wurttemberg antiquities in that place.

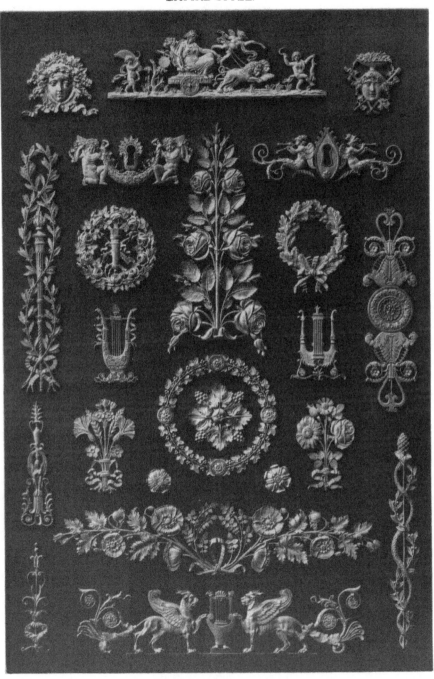

Printed by Bommel & Co., Stuttgart, Germany.

METAL ORNAMENTS.

Plate 90.

XVIIIth. AND XIXth. CENTURIES.

SILK-WEAVING.

————

The silk industry, which flourished in France as early as the XIVth century received a further impetus in the XVIIth and still more in the XVIIIth century by the fashion of covering the walls, and upholstering the furniture, with valuable silk fabrics. This fashion was also helpful to the still older German silk trade.

To supplement the few silk fabrics of the time of Louis XIV., XV. and XVI. shown on Plate 85, we give similar examples of the transition from Louis XVI. to the Empire style. Figs. 1 and 2 are noticeable as inclining to the first style. Apart from traces of Chinese influence we have here the graceful swags and floral festoons, the vases, cornucopiae and torches, the charming and dainty lightness of which are so delightful in the style of Louis XVI., while in the frequent garlands, palms and shields we notice a foreshadowing of the style of the first Republic. Similarly in Fig. 3 the natural flowers remind us of the earlier period, while the rest of the figure and Figs. 4, 5, 6 and 7 are pronouncedly 'Empire'.

——— ———— ————— —

Figs. 1—7. Silk from Specimens in the Royal Museum at Stuttgart.

Fig. 8. From a wall paper (After a photograph).

„ 9. Portion of a ceiling in the Castle of Ludwigsburg (see 'Index').

Fig. 7.

SILK-WEAVING.

Lightning Source UK Ltd.
Milton Keynes UK
UKHW021828160223
417092UK00004B/315